66821683R00076

Made in the USA
Columbia, SC
20 July 2019

## *Z*

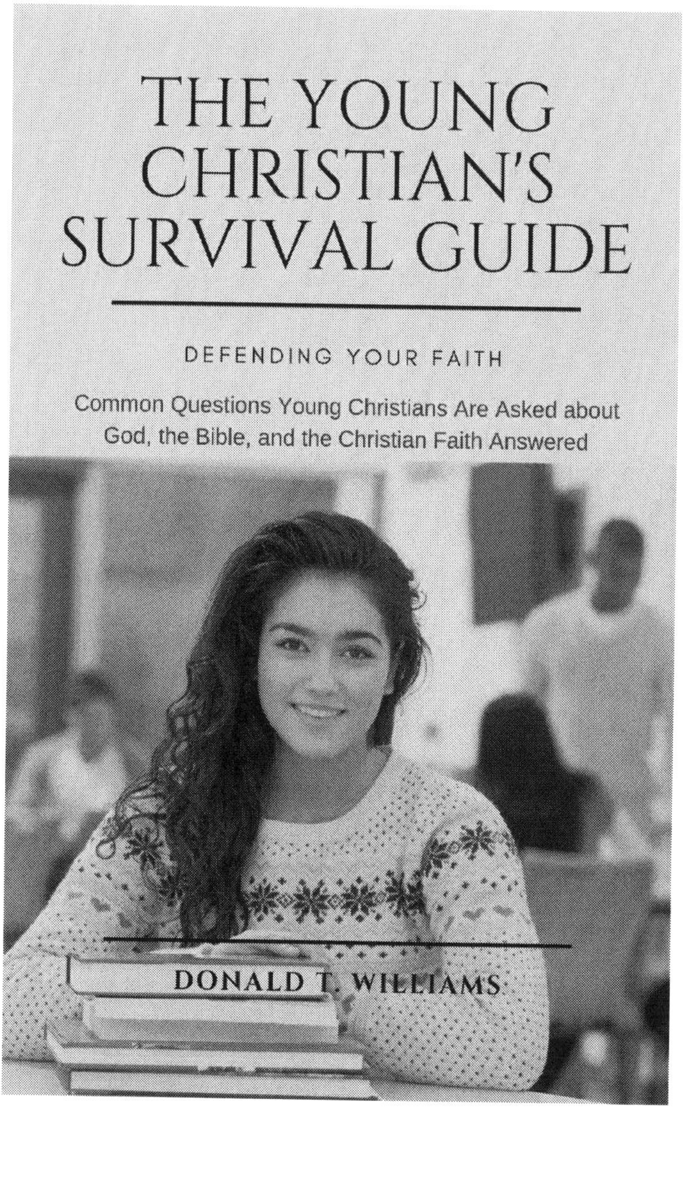
THE YOUNG CHRISTIAN'S SURVIVAL GUIDE
DEFENDING YOUR FAITH
Common Questions Young Christians Are Asked about God, the Bible, and the Christian Faith Answered
DONALD T. WILLIAMS

# THE YOUNG CHRISTIAN'S SURVIVAL GUIDE

## Common Questions Young Christians Are Asked about God, the Bible, and the Christian Faith Answered

DONALD T. WILLIAMS

Christian Publishing House
Cambridge, Ohio

# CHRISTIAN PUBLISHING HOUSE

CONSERVATIVE CHRISTIAN BOOKS

APOLOGETIC DEFENSE OF GOD, THE
FAITH, THE BIBLE, AND CHRISTIANITY

*THE YOUNG CHRISTIAN'S SURVIVAL GUIDE: Common Questions Young Christians Are Asked about God, the Bible, and the Christian Faith Answered* by Donald T. Williams

ISBN-13: **978-1-949586-89-3**

ISBN-10: **1-949586-89-8**

# For All the Youth

# Table of Contents

# Acknowledgements

A version of chapter 13 was originally published in *Christian Research Journal* 40:4 (2017): 42-46. A version of chapter nineteen was originally published in *Christian Research Journal* 39:1 (2016): 46-50. Poems by the author are from *Stars through the Clouds: The Collected Poetry of Donald T. Williams*, 2nd ed. (Toccoa, Ga.: Lantern Hollow Press, 2019).

# Introduction

Nobody can be a Christian whose brain is not turned off without encountering lots of questions. We get bombarded by them from friends, social media, websites, and our own minds. Often, they come with a hostile or suspicious tone that can be as upsetting as the question itself.

If we love Jesus, we don't want our friends to be kept from Him by a lack of answers, and the more we love Jesus, the more we may be bothered by a lack of answers ourselves. And sometimes our church, our parents, our Sunday-School teachers, and our youth leaders can seem as clueless as we are.

When I was in high school, I was bothered by a lot of questions and bothered even more by the attitude some people in my church had toward the ones I was asking: "If you were spiritual you would not be asking that. You just need to read your Bible more and pray harder." That is not the kind of response I was expecting from people who actually have the truth. It was doing more to push me away from the Lord than my friends' skepticism and my own doubts. How could Christianity be true if the people most committed to it were so insecure in their beliefs as to be threatened by my questions?

You will not get that kind of response here. I was blessed to have one good Christian friend who cared as much about the truth as I did, so I didn't face the challenges alone. I was also blessed by the Lord, helping us find people like C. S. Lewis and Francis Schaeffer, who could help us with the answers. Maybe the most important thing Lewis and Schaeffer did for us was just give us permission to be Christians who kept their minds in gear. They showed us that "intelligent Christian" was not an oxymoron. And so we found that there were not only answers to our questions but good answers. We learned to trust Jesus not just as a crutch in our religion but as the Lord of life who was the source of reality and thus the key to real truth about the real world.[1]

I want you to have a solid place where you can stand with real confidence in your own faith. I want you to be able to provide answers to

---

[1] For more about how I made those discoveries and the Christian worldview to which they opened my eyes, see my book *An Encouraging Thought: The Christian Worldview in the Writings of J. R. R. Tolkien* (Cambridge, OH: Christian Publishing House, 2018). See also *Inklings of Reality: Essays toward a Christian Philosophy of Letters* (Lynchburg: Lantern Hollow Press, 2012), esp. the introduction and chapter 1.

your friends that can help them find the same place and put their trust in Jesus as the Way, the Truth, and the Life. So I am going to ask and try to answer some of the more important questions that I hear the most today from skeptics and Christians alike. As you think through them with me, I hope they will help you understand Jesus better and I hope that will help you love Him more. I hope they will reveal Him as the One who really does deserve your trust, your devotion, and your obedience. I know He deserves mine.

I will start with a question that is doubly basic: "You claim the Bible is inspired because it says it is, right (2 Tim. 3:16)? Isn't that circular reasoning?" It is basic in that God's having revealed Himself to us in Christ, and having given us access to that revelation by inspiring the Bible to give us accurate knowledge of it, is the only way we can claim to have legitimate knowledge about God at all—knowledge that would not just let us know He must exist but let us *know Him.* The first chapter then nails down why we can trust the Bible and does it by explaining that we trust it on the authority of Christ, which is grounded in His resurrection from the Dead. Understanding why we believe that Jesus is the Son of God turns out to be the key to why we should trust the Bible. That lets us simultaneously cover the two most important facts and the two most foundational facts we will deal with. (That is why chapter 1 is the longest.) So, chapter one is the foundation on which everything else in the book rests.

The subsequent chapters deal with other questions that arise about the nature of the Bible and how we should relate to it, and then what it has to say about some of the hot issues of our day. The Bible gives good answers to the questions we should be asking, answers that have been caricatured by its enemies. Hopefully, those chapters will help us cut through the clutter and be able to hear the revolutionary, life-changing message of the Bible once again so that we can embrace it with understanding ourselves and help others do so too. If we can do that, we will be better able to obey Jesus' final request—to go into all the world and make disciples of every nation.

So let's begin.

# CHAPTER 1

## "You claim the Bible is inspired because it says it is, right (2 Tim. 3:16)? Isn't that circular reasoning?"

This is a very good question. Unfortunately, many Christians *are* guilty of circular reasoning on this issue. They quote 2 Timothy 3:16 as if that settled it: "All Scripture is inspired by God and profitable for teaching, for reproof, for correction, for training in righteousness." They understand correctly that that the Apostle Paul is claiming that the Bible is more than just words about God; it is the Word *of* God. The word translated "inspired," *theopneustos*, means literally "God-breathed," and it is applied to the *graphe*, which literally means the writings—ink on parchment. Paul is claiming that the words of Scripture, even though they were written by human authors, are as good as if God had spoken them Himself. That is why we can trust them completely and why they are profitable for teaching, reproof, correction, and training in righteousness.

Christians who base their belief in the inspiration of Scripture on that verse have understood what Paul was claiming very accurately. There is only one problem: If you did not already believe the Bible was inspired, why should you believe what Paul is telling you about its inspiration? If we accepted books as inspired by God just because they claimed to be, we would have to accept the Koran and the Book of Mormon as inspired Scripture. But then we would have a number of very different, indeed, contradictory ideas about God and salvation all claiming to be from Him. That is not a logically valid way to proceed.

Fortunately, even though many Christians do make this logical mistake (the fallacy of circular reasoning or "begging the question"), the case for the inspiration and truth of the Christian Scriptures does not depend on it. There is a very good non-circular case that can be made for the inspiration of the Bible. Christians need to know about it, and non-Christians need to respond to it instead of committing their own fallacy by just refuting the weaker argument. (That would be the straw man fallacy.)

# THE NON-CIRCULAR CASE FOR INSPIRATION

The non-circular case for the inspiration of the Bible has the following basic steps. This argument, unlike the circular one, is formally valid. Therefore, we will need to break each of the steps down in detail to see if they stand up. If they do, then the conclusion deserves acceptance. (I will spend a lot of time on Step II because it also gives us the opportunity to answer another pretty important question: **What is the basis for our belief that Jesus was raised from the dead?** You will see that it is not only supremely important in itself but the foundation for everything else.) Here are the steps:

I. The Gospels are **historically reliable** documents.

II. Based on the historical evidence, **Jesus rose from the dead.**

III. If Jesus rose from the dead, then His claims to be **the Son of God** must be accepted.

IV. If Jesus is the Son of God, then **what He taught is true.**

V. Jesus **taught that Scripture is true** down to its jots and tittles.

VI. Therefore, **we accept Scripture as inspired** on the **authority of Jesus established historically**—not just because it claims to be inspired in 2 Tim. 3:16.

OK, let's see how well these claims stand up.

# THE GOSPELS ARE HISTORICALLY RELIABLE DOCUMENTS.

Note that we are not claiming in step one that the Gospels are inspired or inerrant. That would be to fall back into the circular argument. We are only claiming *at this point* that they are basically reliable historical documents. That is, they might have some minor errors or inconsistencies, but they are generally telling the truth about what happened in the First Century. They are as reliable as any other good historical account.

How can we know that the Gospels are basically trustworthy? There are five well established criteria used by historians to evaluate historical testimony in documents and by lawyers to evaluate legal testimony in court. They are used because they have been found by much practical experience over many years of use to be reliable tools for discerning when witnesses are telling the truth. In each case, the Gospels meet the criteria. They pass the test with flying colors.

The first criterion is **proximity to the event.** Were you there? Were you physically placed where you could see the event you are testifying about? I.e., did you actually see the cars as they crashed into each other, or did you just look up when you heard the bang? If it is the latter, then your testimony is really worthless in trying to determine whose fault the accident was. In the case of a historical document, did its author even live in a time when he could have been there at the event he records? If not, the testimony is only hearsay. O.K., how does this apply to the Gospels? In the case of the Gospels, three of them were written by eyewitnesses, and the other one (Luke) by a person who did research and interviewed several people who were eyewitnesses. And they were all written within one generation of the life of Christ.[2] The traditional attributions of the Gospels to Apostles and their associates goes back to within a generation or so of the writers themselves and were never seriously questioned until a skeptical age began to look at the documents with an anti-supernatural bias.

Skeptical views of the Gospels require there to have been a long process of evolution whereby the supposedly simple Jesus of history was gradually transformed into the supernatural Jesus of legend, with the Gospels as we have them representing a late stage in that process. But in reality, that process never had time to take place. For example, Acts is Luke volume two, and it ends with Paul still under house arrest in Rome, no later than about AD 64. That places Luke's Gospel even earlier, around, say, AD 60. That was only thirty years after the crucifixion and resurrection of Christ. There were still too many people around who would have remembered what had actually happened for Luke to have gotten away with fabricating a supernatural Christ out of the supposedly simple Jesus of history. There is not one shred of physical evidence of an earlier source giving us a different Jesus from the one in the Gospels. Furthermore, all four of the canonical Gospels (and no others) were already being quoted *as Scripture* by the Apostolic Fathers before the end of the First Century. The Apostolic Fathers were the first generation of church leaders after the Apostles themselves, many of whom had actually known Apostles. They assume without argument that their readers will accept those documents as Scripture, which means they had to have already been in circulation for

---

[2] If you want to see a more thorough sampling of the evidence that the canonical Gospels were written by eyewitnesses within one generation of the events, see books like F. F. Bruce, *The New Testament Documents: Are they Reliable?* (Downers Grove, IL: 1960) and Richard Bauckham, *Jesus and the Eyewitnesses: The Gospels as Eyewitness Testimony* (Grand Rapids: Eerdmans, & Cambridge: Cambridge Univ. Pr., 2006).

some time. The notion of a gradual evolution of the simple historical Jesus into the divine Christ just does not fit the historical facts.

This does not by itself prove that the men who wrote the Gospels were telling the truth. We need the other criteria to establish that. But it means they could have been telling the truth, and because they were there, we have to take their testimony seriously. It is the first step in establishing their reliability.

The second criterion is **multiple attestation.** You want eyewitness accounts, and you want more than one of them so their testimony can be compared and thus corroborated. Here we have an excellent sample of witnesses to evaluate: the four Gospel writers themselves, the Apostles Paul, Peter, and James in their epistles, and the multiple witnesses interviewed by Luke in the research he did for his account. That is more direct testimony than practically any other event in ancient history can boast!

Skeptics often complain that all of these sources come from Christians and argue that we should therefore discount them. But surely that is an unfair expectation. Who else would have been motivated to write about these events? Those in direct personal contact with them would either have become followers of Christ motivated to share the facts about Him or enemies of Christ wanting to suppress them. It is hardly shocking that Christians were the ones who wanted to talk about what had happened. Many events of ancient history are attested by only one source. The life of Christ is the best attested event of ancient history.

The third criterion is maybe the most important: **consistency**—and it has to be the right kind of consistency. You want multiple accounts that are *consistent* but not *identical.* Why? If the witnesses contradict each other, then obviously that is a problem. Only one of them at most can be telling the truth, and which one? But if they all say exactly the same thing, that is just as big a problem. Two people observing the same event from different angles are going to see the same thing but see it a little differently. If all of your witnesses say *exactly* the same thing, you suspect them of having gotten together to fix their testimony. And their motive for doing that is probably that they are colluding and have some agenda other than simply telling the truth as each of them saw it. You suspect they are trying to hide something. So you want their testimony to be consistent, but not identical. That is, you want there to be *discrepancies*, but not *contradictions.*

Discrepancies but not contradictions? That is exactly what the Gospels give us! Skeptical scholars always emphasize the discrepancies as if they *were* contradictions. We must not be intimidated by that tactic. For

example, take the question of how many angels were present at the tomb after the resurrection. Luke and John have two; Matthew and Mark only mention one. Well, if there were two angels, there was one. You cannot have two without having one! If Matthew or Mark had said that there was one and *only* one, we would have a problem; one version of the story at least would be wrong. But the discrepancy is not a contradiction; it leaves the two accounts compatible though not identical. The fact that two of the witnesses only mention one of the angels—the one who spoke—actually *increases* the credibility of all four accounts rather than diminishing it, for anyone who understands how legal and historical evidence actually works. It shows we have independent testimony that is ultimately compatible rather than people just repeating the same account.

A fourth criterion is that **testimony that is embarrassing** to the witness gains credibility. These last two criteria depend on well-established truths of human psychology. People like to make themselves look better; they hate to make themselves look bad. So if they are going to doctor their story, it is almost always in ways that are to their own advantage. Nobody goes out of his way to change his story to his own disadvantage. Well, how do the disciples come across in the Gospel narratives? They portray themselves as clueless cowards. The first witnesses to the resurrection are women—people whom that society did not trust and whose testimony was not even accepted in court. Nobody who was making the story up would ever have written it that way. Normally the only reason for including such embarrassing details is that they are actually true. Testimony that is embarrassing to the witness is therefore usually believable.

Finally, we tend to believe **testimony from hostile witnesses** because the witness has no conceivable motive other than truthfulness for giving it. If my best friend gives me an alibi, it is less impressive than if my worst enemy has to admit that I have one. Well, the New-Testament accounts were all written by Christians, but several of them were written by men who *used* to be as hostile as they could be to the claims of Christ. That very change of perspective is one of the curious things that have to be explained. Paul was the most zealous persecutor of Christians ever. How did he end up as their most zealous spokesman? James the half-brother of Jesus had not believed in Jesus as the Messiah during Jesus' earthly ministry. Now he shows up writing an epistle as a leader of the early church. Thomas said he would not believe in the resurrection unless he could personally examine the wounds from the crucifixion in Jesus' body. None of the clueless disciples was actually expecting Him to rise from the dead. What changed their minds? That is a question to which skeptics ought to give a great deal more attention.

Our **conclusion:** The Gospels are pretty reliable historical documents. They meet all the criteria and cover all the bases: proximity to the event, multiple attestation, the right kind of consistency, embarrassing testimony, testimony from hostile witnesses. We have to take seriously their version of the events and we should generally believe what they tell us unless we have a very good reason not to. What then do they tell us?

## BASED ON THE HISTORICAL EVIDENCE, JESUS ROSE FROM THE DEAD.

Virtually all reputable historians, including secular and skeptical historians, accept and must explain four facts. We are talking about historians with PhDs from accredited universities, not the kind of conspiracy theorists one sees on the History Channel. Not all qualified historians believe in the resurrection, of course, but hardly any trained historian denies the following facts:

A. Jesus lived and was **crucified** by the Roman governor, Pontius Pilate;
B. He was **buried** in a borrowed tomb;
C. Three days later the tomb was **empty**;
D. Almost immediately his followers were **claiming** that **He had risen** and that they had seen him.

Now, if you are playing the game of historical research according to the rules, you have to accept these facts as facts, and then you have to explain them. The simplest explanation is that God raised Jesus from the dead. But of course, that takes a lot of believing, so secular historians have come up with other explanations that do not involve a miracle. But do any of those other explanations actually succeed in accounting for this rather strange collection of stubborn facts?

All of the secular theories trying to account for these facts have fatal flaws. For example, maybe the women got confused in the early morning light and went to the wrong tomb. When it was empty, they falsely assumed that Jesus had risen from the dead, and that is how the rumor got started. There is only one glaring problem with that explanation. If the women had gone to the wrong tomb, then Jesus' body would still be in the right one. All the Jewish leaders had to do was produce it, and the Christian movement they hated would have been squelched at the outset. Somehow, that never happened.

OK, some people say, maybe Jesus didn't actually die on the Cross. He was only "mostly dead," and so was mistakenly buried, but then He

revived in the cool of the tomb, let Himself out, and freaked out the guards. The problem with this explanation is its complete ignorance of two pretty pertinent facts: the physiology of crucifixion and the details of First-Century tomb construction. Crucifixion was one of the most brutal deaths ever devised by the perversity of human depravity. Jesus was beat to within an inch of his life beforehand. The whole reason Simon of Cyrene was drafted to help carry the cross was that the soldiers in charge were afraid Jesus would not even make to the execution site. Then He had spikes driven through his wrists and ankles and was hanged that way bleeding for hours. The professional executioners certified Him as dead by puncturing his side with a spear. "Blood and water" flowed out—i.e., blood which had separated into its constituent parts, a clinical sign of death. Even if by some miracle Jesus had survived all of this, He would have been in no condition to extricate Himself from the tomb. (Oh, wait, I thought we were trying to get rid of miracles!) It was sealed by a stone that took four strong men (with places to grip) to remove from the outside. Jesus is supposed to stand up on those shattered ankles and push it away with those shattered wrists from the inside? It takes less faith to believe in the resurrection itself.

OK, what if the disciples wanted to believe in the resurrection so badly that they hallucinated it? In the first place, they were not expecting any such thing. It surprised them when it happened. And in the second place, one of them might have had a hallucination, but all of them? A common hallucination experienced by a group that size just has no credibility at all. That is not the way hallucinations work. But that is what you need to explain all the appearances. Well, what about the story the Jews circulated: that the disciples stole the body? But they were scattered and in hiding after the crucifixion and hardly capable of pulling such a caper off. And if they had, they would have known they were lying. Would all of them have suffered persecution, torture, exile, or death for something they knew was a lie? Maybe one might, but all of them?

The resurrection ends up being the only theory that actually accounts for the facts. History is not capable of giving you an absolute proof, but people who believe that Jesus rose from the dead are making a reasonable conclusion from very solid evidence. The evidence, as such, supports them. You must trust your philosophical bias about what could or could not have happened over the actual evidence in order to reject the resurrection. (See chapters 6-7.) If you want to do that, you can, but you cannot then claim that the Christians are the ones who don't care about what the evidence says! You cannot claim that you are the only one who cares about the evidence and they just believe in fairy tales. OK, if you accept the evidence, what follows from it?

## IF JESUS ROSE FROM THE DEAD, THEN HIS CLAIMS TO BE THE SON OF GOD MUST BE ACCEPTED.

One of the reasons why the case for the resurrection is so convincing is that we are talking about *Jesus*. A resurrection from the dead takes a lot of believing. But this is not some random dude in some miscellaneous place that we are saying rose from the dead. This is a man whose coming had been prepared by Providence and predicted by prophecy for two thousand years. This is a man whose friends kept asking themselves, "What manner of man *is* this?" and being compelled to answer that question in theistic terms. This is the reassertion of a life that had already shown itself to be sovereign over life and death. If ever there was a man about whom we could believe such a thing, it is this man: It is Jesus of Nazareth.

The resurrection then is not just a weird happening. It is the high point of God's testimony to the human race about Jesus. It begins in the prophets who predicted His coming, rises to a climax in the Gospels which narrate it, and continues in the Epistles which explain it: "This is my beloved Son, in whom I am well pleased. Listen to Him!" (Mat. 17:5). The resurrection is the keystone of that testimony. It seals and nails down the truth about who Jesus was: "Thou art the Christ, the Son of the living God." It is the ultimate vindication of Jesus' own claim that "I and the Father are one." It assures us that Jesus was indeed nothing less than what He claimed to be: God manifested in human flesh.

## IF JESUS IS THE SON OF GOD, THEN WHAT HE TAUGHT IS TRUE.

The resurrection proves that Jesus is the Christ, the Son of the living God. It proves that He is the Way, the truth, and the Life. Therefore, if we accept the conclusion that the resurrection happened, we must accept everything that Jesus taught as true.

## JESUS TAUGHT THAT SCRIPTURE IS TRUE DOWN TO ITS JOTS AND TITTLES.

One of the consistent points that Jesus made, attested in multiple statements from multiple sources, is that the Bible is the Word of God, that it is true, and that it should be trusted completely. Because of the Bible's ultimate Source (God), there is a metaphysical necessity of its statements proving true. The universal explanation of why important things in Christ's life happened is "But this has happened that the Scriptures might be

fulfilled" (Mark 14:49). This necessity reaches all the way down to the "jots and tittles"—Hebrew diacritical markings analogous to our English dotting of the i and crossing of the t. "Not the smallest letter or stroke shall pass away from the Law until all is fulfilled" (Mat. 5:18). And in case you missed it, "The Scriptures cannot be broken" (John 10:35b).

Now, Jesus was of course speaking about the Old Testament. The New Testament had not yet been written when He said those things. But He commissioned His Apostles to speak for Him, and their writings were understood as completing the Old Testament by having the same kind of inspiration it did (See chapter 2). Jesus promised the disciples that the Holy Spirit would teach them all things and help them remember what had happened accurately (John 14:26). Peter counts Paul's letters as being on the same level as the Old-Testament Scriptures (2 Pet. 3:16) and affirms that the Apostles did not follow cleverly devised tales but were eyewitnesses of Christ's majesty, and that God used this to "make the prophetic word more sure" (2 Pet. 1:16-21). The New Testament then brings the Old to completion and confirms its message. Having the completed Bible makes us even more sure about the inspiration and truth of each part. Ultimately, we accept it as true because Jesus did, and we trust Jesus.

## THEREFORE, WE ACCEPT SCRIPTURE AS INSPIRED ON THE AUTHORITY OF JESUS ESTABLISHED HISTORICALLY—NOT JUST BECAUSE IT CLAIMS TO BE INSPIRED IN 2 TIM. 3:16.

Christians accept the Bible as the Word of God, not just because it claims to be the Word of God, but because Jesus taught us that it is. Aren't those words of Jesus in the Bible themselves? Yes. But we do not accept *them* as true because we had *already* assumed that the Bible is perfectly true. We used the normal criteria of historical research to realize that the Bible is a basically reliable historical document that gives us a believable portrait of Jesus and account of His words. This gives us a compelling basis for accepting His authority. And then from His words we learn that the Bible is *more* than just a good historical document: It is the inspired and inerrant Word of God. The inspiration of the Bible, the written Word of God, depends on the authority of Jesus, the living Word of God. Indeed. For Christians who understand their faith, *everything* depends on Jesus. For He is the Christ, the Son of the living God.

# CHAPTER 2

## "You claim the Bible was inspired, but there was no inspired list of which books that is true of. So how can we know which ones to trust?"

The Bible is a remarkable book. It is actually a library of sixty-six books written by some forty different authors who lived a thousand and a half years apart. Prophets of God in the Old Testament and Apostles of Jesus and their friends in the New Testament not only told us about their experiences with God, but we believe were inspired to give us the actual Word of God. But the Table of Contents in the front of your Bible wasn't actually part of any of those books. It was added by the modern editors and translators. So how do we know which books are supposed to be in the Bible, when none of them actually contains a divinely approved list? A list of the books approved and accepted as part of Scripture is known as a *canon.* The canon—not the Bible itself, but its table of contents, the list of which books were part of it—was created after the fact by the church. Or, more accurately, the church was led to recognize which books God has inspired to lead it to the truth and to reject those which He had not.

How did the churches recognize these books? What criteria did they use? How do we know they got the list right? It would be nice if the last biblical book to be written (Revelation) had included an inspired list, but it didn't. Why not?

The reason is that Christianity was not *primarily* based on a book. It was based on a Person, and on the proclamation of the Good News about that Person, made (initially) by the people who had known Him directly. Then, because a book (what we call the Old Testament) was trusted by that person (Jesus) and was understood authoritatively to point to Jesus, it was accepted as Scripture by the early church. And because Jesus was Himself the completion of the revelation of God that had been begun in the Old Testament, He commissioned his closest associates to complete the written record of that revelation by writing the New Testament.

# THE OLD TESTAMENT

The early Christians, who were at first all Jews, simply took over the canon of the Old Testament (the Hebrew Scriptures) from Judaism. They did so because Jesus Himself had taught them that those Scriptures "bear witness of Me" (John 5:29) and that "all things which were written about Me in the Law of Moses and the Prophets and the Psalms must be fulfilled" (Luke 24:44). He had taught them that the Hebrew Scriptures were inspired and completely trustworthy down to their finest details: "Not the smallest letter or stroke shall pass away from the Law until all is fulfilled" (Mat. 5:18). He had taught them that "The Scriptures cannot be broken" (John 10:35b). So, the earliest Christians accepted the Jewish Bible as Scripture precisely *because* their faith was in not a book but a Person—and that Person had told them to receive the Old Testament as the Word of God.

All Christians then accept the thirty-nine books of the Old Testament—what Jews call the *Tanakh*, an acronym for the Hebrew words for the Law, the Prophets, and the Writings—as Scripture. (The Hebrew Bible organizes and numbers the books differently, but it is essentially the same collection of writings.) But there is a handful of additional books known as the "Apocrypha" which are also accepted by the Roman Catholic and Eastern Orthodox churches: 1 and 2 Esdras, Tobit, Judith, The Wisdom of Solomon, Ecclesiasticus, Baruch, The Song of the Three Holy Children, Susanna, Bel and the Dragon, and 1 and 2 Maccabees. Where did they come from, and why aren't they accepted by everyone?

A couple of centuries before Christ, Jews living outside of Palestine had lost enough fluency in the Hebrew language to feel the need for a translation of the Old Testament into Greek. That translation was known as the Septuagint, for the seventy rabbis who according to legend had worked on it. It contained some extra books, sometimes known as "the Septuagint plus," which had been written later than the books of the standard Hebrew Old Testament. They were accepted by Hellenistic (i.e., Greek-speaking) Jews, but never became part of the official Hebrew Bible used in the Holy Land.

Because the Gentile Christians who could not read Hebrew naturally used the Septuagint as their Old Testament, some early Christians came to accept those books. But clearly the Bible used by Jesus when He was teaching in the synagogues of the Holy Land would have been the stricter Hebrew Old Testament—and that would therefore have been the Bible He was referring to when He authorized the use of the Old Testament as Christian Scripture. This led church fathers like Athanasius, one of the

greatest theologians, and Jerome, the greatest Bible scholar of that day, to distinguish between the Apocrypha and the rest of the Old Testament.

The Old-Testament Apocryphal writings, according to Athanasius and Jerome, were good books worthy to be read for devotional purposes, they said, but they should not be used as the basis of doctrine. They continued to be included in Bibles on that basis (though with the distinction often forgotten) until the Reformation. Then the Reformers, concerned as they were with biblical authority, restored the distinction very strictly, which eventually led to Protestant Bibles being printed without the apocryphal books. Printing them as part of the Bible does not exactly encourage people to maintain the important distinction!

The bottom line is that the thirty-nine books of the Old Testament according to the Masoretic Text of the Hebrew Bible are accepted by all Christians as undisputed Scripture. While some accept the Apocrypha, it is best to follow the practice of Jerome and the Reformers and read those books but not treat them as inspired Scripture. That accounts for the Old Testament. What about the New?

## THE NEW TESTAMENT

At first, the church's Bible was the Old Testament as interpreted by Jesus and His Apostles, who were authorized by Jesus to hand on the Good News about Jesus in its definitive form after His ascension to Heaven. An Apostle had to be someone who was an eyewitness of the Resurrection—starting of course with the eleven surviving Disciples. Paul was qualified by having seen the risen Lord on the road to Damascus.

At first the living voice of the Apostles was sufficient as a guide to understanding the Hebrew Bible and its witness to Christ. As the church spread and not all congregations had a resident Apostle, the first New-Testament documents came about with Paul writing letters to churches he was not able to visit at the moment, either dealing with problems or issues they were facing (e.g., Galatians, the Corinthian letters) or giving them systematic teaching (Romans, Ephesians). Churches kept these letters and even shared them (Col. 4:16). By the sixties of the First Century, it is clear that no less an authority than Peter was thinking of them as part of Scripture alongside the Old Testament (2 Pet. 3:16). By the middle of the First Century there were written Gospels. Luke, writing about AD 60, makes it clear that he was not the first to write one (Luke 1:1-4). As the original Apostles neared the end of their lives and realized that Jesus might not return until after they were gone, they became concerned that the church needed to have their teaching in permanent form. So Peter promised to be

"diligent that at any time after my departure you will be able to call these things to mind" (2 Pet. 1:15).

As a result of this process, by the end of the First Century the churches were using a collection of such writings by Apostles or those writing under their direct supervision (e.g., Mark, Luke) as Scripture alongside the Hebrew Bible. The Apostolic Fathers are the first generation of leaders after the Apostles themselves: men like Ignatius of Antioch, Clement of Rome, Papias, and Polycarp. In their own writings, they are already citing most of our New Testament, including the four canonical Gospels (and no others) *as Scripture*. Impressively, they make no argument for the Scriptural status of these works, showing that it had already been accepted without controversy by most of the churches in that day. It is important to know this, because skeptics often point out that there was no definitive list of books accepted by everyone as part of the New Testament and identical to the one we have today until the Fourth Century. But the fact is that for all practical purposes a functioning canon pretty close to the one we use today was in place by the end of the First Century AD.

Why did it take until the Fourth Century for the canon to be completely settled and finally closed? There were a few books for which a universal consensus was slower to form. For example, Hebrews is unlike most of the other Epistles in not stating its author. Was it by Paul or one of his associates? Some people were not sure. Revelation was hard to understand. (It still is!) Second and Third John were so small that they may have gotten lost in the shuffle. Then there were a couple of early writings, such as *The Shepherd of Hermas* and *The Didache* that some people considered including. Finally, in 367 AD, Athanasius in a letter is the first to give a list which is exactly the same one we use today.[3] By the end of the century with the acceptance of Jerome's Latin "Vulgate" translation, the New-Testament canon was closed.

## CRITERIA OF CANONICITY

How did the church arrive at our list of twenty-seven New-Testament books? It was accomplished through an informal process of consensus building. We don't have minutes of the deliberations, and there was no one council where the leaders set down and worked out what the canon was going to be anyway. But there were four important criteria that were used in the sifting process: apostolicity, universality, orthodoxy, and

[3] F. F. Bruce, *The Canon of Scripture* (Downers Grove , Il.: InterVarsity Press, 1988), p. 208.

potency. **1. Apostolicity:** was the book written by an Apostle or by a close associate of an Apostle working as it were under his supervision, under the umbrella of his apostolic authority? **2. Universality:** was the book accepted everywhere and by everyone? (This took the longest to fall into place.) **3. Orthodoxy:** did the book teach the Gospel as it had been understood since the beginning, since apostolic times? Did it teach "the faith once delivered to the saints?" (Jude 1:3). **4. Potency:** Did the book impress itself on the conscience of the church as coming with the power of the Holy Spirit?

Books that passed all four tests were accepted with confidence. All but a handful of our New Testament books, and no others, had already found such acceptance by the end of the First Century. When there were questions, such as the authorship of Hebrews, universal acceptance took a little longer. But the canonization of a collection of apostolic writings that would become the New Testament was given impetus by the Apostles themselves, as with Peter's attribution of Scriptural authority to the writings of Paul. The early Christians were the only ones in a position to make the call, and there is no good reason to think they got it wrong. There is simply no other document with a credible claim to having passed all four tests that they could have included. *The Shepherd of Hermas* and *The Didache* never claimed to be by Apostles, and the so-called apocryphal Gospels were all written far too late (Second-Century or later).[4]

## CONCLUSION

Some people love to ask, "What if we discovered a manuscript of a long-lost Epistle, like Paul's Epistle to the Laodiceans or the missing letter to Corinth?" Well, what if we did? It would be a very interesting discovery, no doubt; but how could we ever at this distance in time be certain of its authenticity? It is probably too late for any new books to be accepted in any case. The ship of the canon sailed over sixteen hundred years ago. Besides, it is a purely hypothetical question which should not stop us from using the real Bible we actually have, the one that the whole church has accepted as being from God for two thousand years. The bottom line is that we have no sound reason not to accept it too.

[4] For further information on the formation of the canon see Paul Copan, *"How Do You Know You're not Wrong?" Responding to Objections that Leave Christian Speechless* (Grand Rapids: Baker, 2005), pp. 218-40.

# CHAPTER 3

# "With so many different copies of manuscripts that have 400,000+ variants (errors), how can we even know what the Bible says?"

This is a question you hear a lot. The Bible was copied more often than any other book. We have literally thousands of manuscripts of it that have survived (about 5,836 for the Greek New Testament alone), copied by hand before the invention of the printing press and going all the way back to the Second Century. The scribes who wrote them were accomplished and professional copyists, but sometimes, being human, they lost their concentration and made mistakes, ranging from what today we would call a typo to more serious errors: leaving out a line, or copying one twice, or even mistaking a marginal notation for part of the original text. So it is an understandable question: Does the end result of all that copying give us a text we can *rely on* to be what the authors originally wrote? And how can we tell whether it does or not?

## WHAT IS AT STAKE

There is a science called "textual criticism" that is devoted to answering such questions. It has developed a number of reliable criteria that work together to let us determine which of two different readings (called "variants") is the original wording. When combined with the wealth of information we have about the manuscripts of the New Testament, they give us pretty much 99% certainty about the original wording. And almost all the discrepancies that remain are trivial, with no effect on the meaning of the passages in question and no impact at all on the doctrines being taught by them.

For example, I open my Greek New Testament at random and my eye lights on Luke 12:1. I translate as follows: "Meanwhile, with a crowd of so many thousands gathered together that they were stepping on each other, He started saying to his disciples, first of all, 'Watch out for the leaven, that is, the hypocrisy, of the Pharisees.'" A footnote at the bottom of the page informs me that some manuscripts say, "the leaven, that is, the hypocrisy,

of the Pharisees," and others say, "The leaven of the Pharisees, which is hypocrisy." The second group of manuscripts is larger, but both groups include some fairly early papyri. The editors chose the first reading as the original, probably because they think it is more likely that some scribe smoothed out its slightly more convoluted syntax than that he went out of his way to create it out of a smoother original reading. But the point is that it really doesn't matter. The meaning of the verse is exactly the same either way. Luke's message to us—and therefore God's—comes through loud and clear. Almost all the cases where there is any real doubt at all about the original wording turn out to be pretty much like this one. There are a few problems like the ending of Mark's Gospel that are more difficult. Nevertheless, not a single doctrine of Scripture depends on the choice of one textual variant over another. This is a problem that looks serious at first but turns out not to be a big deal at all. You will see this when we look at the abundance of the evidence we have and the criteria by which it is evaluated.

### THE NATURE OF THE EVIDENCE

Sorting through all of those manuscripts, noting the places where they have small differences, and choosing the reading that best reflects the original wording is a huge undertaking because the evidence is so abundant—almost 5,836 manuscripts of all or part of the Greek New Testament, plus other evidence from translations, Scripture passages quoted in service books, etc. But while the sheer volume of evidence might seem daunting, it is important to realize that the very weight of it all is actually a very good thing. We have more—much more—to go on than we do for any other ancient book. Many of those other books have only a handful of manuscripts that have survived, or sometimes even only one, and often the oldest is a thousand years removed from the original—yet we do not seriously doubt that we essentially know what Homer or Plato wrote. With the New Testament we have thousands of copies, going *almost* all the way back to the originals. If you add to the abundance of evidence a number of well-thought-out criteria for evaluating that evidence, you can see that our confidence in the accuracy of the text we have today is fully justified. How then do we judge between the different readings when we find them?

## HOW TO EVALUATE THE EVIDENCE

No one criterion determines the outcome. Rather, many different factors are weighed. The first, and least important, is **how many manuscripts** give the reading in question? Supporters of the so-called "majority text" or *textus receptus* (the text behind the King James Bible) fail to understand that by itself, a large number means nothing. If a mistake

was made in a manuscript that happened to be in a place where many copies were made from it, say, five hundred, that is not five hundred and one witnesses to the wording of the original; it is only one. All the five hundred copies are just repeating the testimony of the one copy from which they were made, not adding to it. To discern what was happening in its copying and how it relates to the original, we need the other criteria.

The second criterion is **the age of the manuscript**. All other things being equal, the older a manuscript is, the more likely it is to reflect the original wording accurately because there has been less opportunity for corruptions to have found their way into the text. But again, age *by itself* cannot settle the question. What if a manuscript made in the year 300 AD was copied directly from one (which we no longer have) that was made in the year 100, while another manuscript which was done in 200 AD was copied from a manuscript made almost in its own time, and actually has more steps between it and the original manuscript than the copy made a hundred years later? That could easily happen. The first manuscript might actually be the stronger witness even though the second is a hundred years older.

A much bigger factor than the uninitiated might think is the **geographical distribution** of manuscripts with a certain reading. If you think about it, you will realize that a reading that only occurs in manuscripts from one area probably derives from a mistake that was made in an older copy in that location, while a reading that is found all over the old Roman Empire is more likely to reflect what all localities have in common: the original copy from which all other copies were made and distributed. Scribes are not likely to just happen to make the same identical mistake independently in many different locations.

Determining the original reading is not just a matter of weighing manuscripts. You have to know something about the **copying practices** of different schools of scribes and about the **kinds of mistakes** that naturally happen on the rare occasion when one of then nods off. Some of these mistakes happened often enough to have fancy names: *Haplography* occurs when the same word appears twice in the original, say, at the end of two different lines. Then the scribe looks down, sees the second one instead of the first, and picks up copying from there, so the word is only written once (that's what *haplography* means) instead of twice, and the line in between gets skipped. *Dittography* is the opposite—the scribe writes the same word twice instead of once. In Greek handwriting as in English, there are certain letters that could easily be confused with one another when the scribe's eyes are glazing over at the end of a long day of copying. Our confidence in picking a certain reading goes up when we can see how

the other reading was created by a natural mistake. "Aha!" we say: "If this was the original, it would explain where these other variants came from."

There are other scribal tendencies that we know about that give rise to **more sophisticated criteria**. Some scribes were so zealous not to leave anything out that they might add to the actual text what was a marginal note made by the previous scribe in what is now the master copy. Or if a scribe knew of two words or phrases occurring in two different earlier copies, he might include both just to be sure he had gotten the right one. Or if two accounts of the same event or the same saying in two different Gospels were worded slightly differently, the scribe might put both sets of words in both places. So we have the criterion known as *lectio brevior potior*: the shorter reading is (all other factors being equal) to be preferred. On the other hand, a pious scribe who did not understand a passage might think the Apostle could not possibly have written what he sees before him, so he might alter it to what he assumed the writer must have actually said. Hence, we get the maxim *lectio difficilior potior*: the more difficult reading (all other factors being equal) is to be preferred.

It is very important to realize that none of these criteria determines anything by itself. They all have to be factored in together, and when many of them point in the same direction, we are very confident that we have gotten the solution right. The textual critic is trying to create a family tree that shows all the variants eventually going back to the one original reading that explains them all. Merely explaining how it works makes it seem more difficult than it is. In fact, most of the words are not in question to start with, most of the ones that are in question have solutions that we are virtually sure of, and of the few that are still remain, most of those make no essential difference to the meaning of the text. For all practical purposes, we *can* say that we know what the original writings said.

## CONCLUSION

Our warranted confidence that we can still hear the voices of the New-Testament writers after two thousand years is joyous and bracing. Lovers of words find the quest of tracing them through the manuscripts to find their way back to the original text a romantic mystery more fascinating than any case Sherlock Holmes or Miss Marple or the Hardy Boys ever investigated. Those who have mastered the facts of the manuscripts and the criteria for investigating them laid out above will be satisfied that at the end of that quest we still have assurance of reliable access to the truths written down for us by the Prophets and the Apostles.

Sadly, there are people who are only interested in using the existence of variants as an excuse not to engage with the text and be confronted by its truth. You can explain the way textual scholarship actually works to them until you are blue in the face, and they will simply insist on repeating their mantra that we have no idea what was originally written as if they had heard nothing. They are rather like the dwarfs in C.S. Lewis's *The Last Battle*, so afraid of being taken in that they cannot be taken out of the prisons of their own closed minds. One of them inspired me (if you can call it that) to write the following sonnet:

## THE SKEPTIC AND THE TEXT

The Skeptic is usually willfully blind. He or she chooses to ignore the evidence. Right now, we have some world-renowned textual scholars several of which are also Christian apologists. The biggest critic of the Greek New Testament is Agnostic Dr. Bart D. Ehrman. He is one of the top leading textual scholars for the Greek New Testament and early Christianity. He has authored about 30 books on the Text of the New Testament and early Christianity. His book Misquoting Jesus was a New York Times bestseller and has been the go-to source for the Bible critic, skeptics, atheist, Muslims in their attack on the Bible. Ehrman misleads, misinforms, and gives his readers much misinformation. There are many great textual books dealing with Ehrman and there are many very good New Testament and Old Testament textual criticism books as well. A good place to start would be, THE READING CULTURE OF EARLY CHRISTIANITY: The Production, Publication, Circulation, and Use of Books in the Early Christian Church by Edward D. Andrews (ISBN-13: 978-1-949586-84-8).

In our efforts to evangelize, all Christians are commanded to proclaim the Word of God, to teach and make disciples. (Matt. 24:14; 28:19-20; Ac 1:8) What the reader should understand is that we are obligated to witness to others, but we are not responsible for hardened hearts, the unreceptive minds, not to mention willful ignorance. We are obligated to share the Word of God with the intent of making disciples but even Jesus Christ and the apostle Paul could not overcome the will of the unreasonable and the irrational because they were beyond repentance. Simply put, offer your best evidence but do not waste your time on pharisaical minds because this is what Satan wants. If you spend months trying to reason with the unreasonable, imagine how many reasonable minds you will have missed. In addition, just because a person is skeptical or has doubts, this does not make him unreasonable. Give him or her time; however, if they mock, make fun, deride, this is a sign of being unreasonable.

Don't be that skeptic. Follow the quest instead!

I have had the privilege of studying those ancient manuscripts for fifty years, and of seeing a number of them with my own eyes. The most impressive was Codex Sinaiticus,[5] one of the oldest (Fourth Century) complete copies of the New Testament that has survived. I had been reading about it for years, seeing it cited in the footnotes of my Greek New Testament. And there it was, lying unexpectedly under a pane of glass in the British Museum (since moved to the British Library). Each letter was no so much written as drawn with great care. The lines, columns, and margins were almost as straight and uniform as in one of the early printed books (*incunabula*) in the next aisle. Everything I have been saying in this chapter came together at that moment in a rush of gratitude to God for the Apostles who wrote the books, for the scribes who labored so carefully and patiently to copy them for us, and for the teachers who had put me in a position to appreciate it all.

## CODEX SINAITICUS

| | |
|---|---|
| Name | Sinaiticus |
| Sign | א ('Aleph) |
| Text | Old and New Testament |
| Date | c. 330–360 |
| Script | Greek |
| Found | Sinai 1844 |
| Now at | Brit. Libr., Leipzig University, Saint Catherine's Monastery, Russian Nat. Libr. |
| Cite | Lake, K. (1911). Codex Sinaiticus Petropolitanus, Oxford. |
| Size | 38.1 × 34.5 cm (15.0 × 13.6 in) |
| Type | Alexandrian text-type |
| Category | I |
| Note | very close to Papyrus 66 |

5 The two best manuscripts are P75 (175-225 A.D.) and the Vaticanus (350 A.D.). Yes, Codex Sinaiticus is VERY good indeed but Vaticanus is far more superior than even that manuscript.

# CHAPTER 4

## "Why can't the people who wrote the four Gospels get their story straight?"

The early church gave us four different Gospels, four different stories about the life and ministry of Jesus. They are presented as four independent accounts of His life, death, and resurrection. The first three (called the "synoptics") are fairly similar in style. Matthew and Luke may have actually used Mark, and all three culled from the same oral tradition of soundbytes about Jesus' deeds and teachings that were carefully memorized and handed down for the few years between His death and the time when written Gospels were able to be composed. But they also show independence from each other in what they remembered and what they chose to include and to emphasize. John's Gospel was written a bit later, and so it focuses on material that was not already familiar from the first three.

Together the four accounts give us a rich portrait of Jesus that has the depth perception that comes from seeing the same object from different perspectives. That is a good thing. But it also creates the possibility of confusion when two of them report what seems to be the same saying or event slightly differently. If you have a nit-picky and skeptical disposition, it is easy to find "errors" in some of those discrepancies. But are they really *errors*, or is something else going on? That is the question we will try to answer in this chapter.

Here are some examples of the kind of thing we are talking about. At Jesus' baptism by John the Baptist, did the Father's voice from Heaven say, "This is my beloved Son, in whom I am well pleased" (Mat. 3:17) or "You are my beloved Son; in you I am well pleased" (Mark 1:11, Luke 3:22)? In the Sermon on the Mount, did Jesus say, "Blessed are the poor in spirit" (Mat. 5:3), or "Blessed are you poor" (Luke 6:20)? Was that sermon preached on a mountain (Mat. 5:1) or a level place (Luke 6:17)? Did the inscription Pilate hung over the cross say, "This is Jesus, the King of the Jews" (Mat. 27:37) or just "The King of the Jews" (Mark 15:26) or "This is the King of the Jews" (Luke 23:38) or "Jesus the Nazarene, the King of the Jews" (John 19:19)? When the women went to the tomb on Sunday morning, did they meet an angel (Mat. 28:2, Mark 16:5), or two angels (Luke 24:4, John 20:12)?

If you are looking for a reason to distrust the historical accuracy of the Gospel accounts, these and many other such discrepancies look like good excuses. But I will argue that if you look at the material fairly and without a skeptical bias, they are not a problem. Almost all of them have plausible resolutions that have been known for years.[6] On the contrary, far from being a potential stumbling block, they are really a positive good that enriches the stereoscopic depth of our portrait of Jesus and actually enhances our trust in the Gospel writers and the reliability, the factual accuracy, of their accounts.

## INDEPENDENT TESTIMONY

We saw in chapter 1 that when we are evaluating the reliability of eyewitness testimony, whether in a trial or in historical documents, we actually don't want the accounts to be identical. If two witnesses agree word for word, if they say exactly the same thing, that is not something that happens naturally. If they are in court we suspect that have gotten together and agreed in advance on what they were going to say. They almost certainly have some agenda other than just telling the truth as they saw it that motivated them to do that. If they are in historical documents we may suspect that one of them may have just copied the other one. Then we don't really have two independent witnesses corroborating each other—we really only have one, because the second is just repeating what the first one said. In both cases, our level of trust in their testimony then goes down, not up, as a result of their perfect agreement.

The witnesses will support and corroborate each other and increase their credibility, on the other hand, if they give two distinguishable but consistent perspectives on the same event. In such a case there will be *discrepancies* in their accounts, but hopefully not *contradictions*. We applied this to the angels at the tomb in that first discussion: If there were two angels there, then obviously there was one. It's not a contradiction unless the one group says there were two and the other says there was *only* one. A contradiction would be a problem, but a discrepancy that is capable of reasonable harmonization is not. It actually increases the credibility of the witnesses rather than hurting it. This may seem counterintuitive, but

6 Most of those resolutions have been known for a long time; the passages only became a problem when a skeptical age put its negative spin on them. Those interested in pursuing those solutions will find much help in Gleason Archer, *Encyclopedia of Bible Difficulties* (Grand Rapids: Zondervan, 1982) and John W. Haley, *An Examination of the Alleged Discrepancies of the Bible* (1874; rpt. Grand Rapids: Baker, 1977).

that is actually the way it works, as any competent lawyer or historian will be happy to tell you.

Well, the Gospels are full of situations exactly like this. Almost all of them can be harmonized and reconciled easily and plausibly. In fact, so many of them can that we are fully justified in giving the accounts the benefit of the doubt on the few where the answer is not so easy to see right off. The remarkable agreement and honesty of these witnesses, factors that are all over every page but ignored by the nit-pickers, has earned them that level of trust.

## THEMINISTRY OF JESUS

One large group of discrepancies can be eliminated in one fell swoop if we just remember a few basic facts about Jesus' ministry. He was an itinerant preacher. He went around from town to town preaching His message about the Kingdom of God. Almost certainly He re-used some of his material on multiple occasions. Almost certainly He did not compose a new and original sermon on the spot in every single village. And guess what? He was under no obligation to repeat Himself verbatim whenever He recycled His material! I have preached the same sermon to different congregations myself on more than one occasion, and I can guarantee you that if you compared the transcripts, they would say the same thing but contain enough differences in wording to convince a liberal biblical critic that I was two different people! Such a thought process and such a conclusion have no more credibility when applied to Jesus' preaching than they do when applied to mine. Small discrepancies in those who report the wording of His sayings are what we should *expect* to find. It is evidence of good reporting, not bad.

Add to that the fact that Jesus would have preached in Aramaic to be readily understood by his usual audiences of uneducated Jews, and what He said then had to be translated into Greek to be available to the largest possible audience (which would include Gentiles) for the written Gospels. You can only obsess over small differences in wording if you simply refuse to let common sense be a player in the game of Gospel interpretation. Scholars who have not forgotten their common sense distinguish between the *ipsissima verba*, the exact words, which we do not have (they were in Aramaic) and the *ipsissima vox*, the genuine voice of Jesus, which we do have faithfully preserved in the Greek of the four Gospels. At no point do those small verbal differences keep us from hearing, and hearing accurately, what Jesus wanted to say to us.

# JUST THE FACTS

The Gospel writers ought to have earned our trust on the factual details too. Was Jesus' most famous sermon delivered on a mountain (Matthew 5:1) or a level place (Luke 6:17)? We have already noted the great possibility, indeed, likelihood, that it was preached more than once. But even if Matthew and Luke are describing the same event, there is reason to give them the benefit of the doubt. You can visit the "mount" of the Sermon today. I have done so. We actually know where it was. There is a chapel on top of it now, The Church of the Beatitudes. But the topography of the mountain is what matters. It starts uphill from the shores of the Sea of Galilee, goes up for a while, levels off, and then goes up some more to the top. The level place (or "plain") halfway up is the only place where a crowd could have gathered for the sermon. So all you have to do to solve the difficulty is just go look at the spot. You should do so someday. When you do, be sure to read the Sermon on the Mount while sitting in that level place on the mountain, with the descendants of the original birds of the air still circling over your head and the offspring of the original lilies of the field still growing at your feet—just as their ancestors were when Jesus spoke those words two thousand years ago.

Mountain? Level place? Which is it? Both. Both, plain and simple. Both writers are speaking accurately, just emphasizing different aspects of the same geological feature. Entire forests of trees have given their lives to create the reams of paper on which scholars have debated this difference between the two accounts. All they would have had to do was go and look. Modern liberal biblical critics remind you of the legendary medieval scholastic theologians debating the number of teeth in a horse's mouth with all kinds of obscure citations and clever arguments, when they all had horses tied up outside and it never occurred to a single one of them to go out and count the teeth.

The order of events is another issue where people get all tied up in knots unnecessarily. The gospels often seem to be organized topically as much as chronologically. "OK, now I'm going to give you a big sample of the kinds of things Jesus said. Now I'm going to give you a bunch of miracle stories, about the kinds of things He did." The baptism at the beginning of His public ministry and Passion Week at the end of it are easy to nail down but trying to construct a strict chronology of everything in between

is difficult. That doesn't mean that the events we read about did not happen or the words were not said.[7]

## CONCLUSION

I cannot resolve every difficulty. Nobody today knows enough to do that. Did Jesus cleanse the Temple at the beginning of his ministry (as the synoptics imply) or near the end (John), or did he do it twice? I'm not one hundred percent sure. But I don't need to be. Over and over again I have seen situations where the critics were one hundred percent sure that one at least of the Gospels had gotten something wrong, and it turns out that the Gospel writers were not only right but careful and precise.

There is a pattern there! When you have a pattern that strong, the smart bet is to trust the men who were there and who have demonstrated their reliability time after time. They have a way better track record than their critics do. So I'm going to remember the non-circular argument for the inspiration of Scripture from chapter one and recognize that the few remaining difficulties that I can't solve are no reason at all not to accept that conclusion. Why would I expect to be able to resolve everything two thousand years after the fact? That would be to dismiss my common sense and become like the critics. Not a smart move.

---

[7] For further discussion of these issues and their resolution see Paul Copan, *"That's Just Your Interpretation": Responding to Skeptics Who Challenge Your Faith* (Grand Rapids: Baker, 2001), pp. 179-87.

# CHAPTER 5

# "Didn't the Council of Nicaea just arbitrarily pick the books for the Bible that they agreed with and suppress all the rest with political power?"

This idea is a very popular one. Most people who believe it have no idea that it has its origins in a conspiracy theory worthy of the History Channel that was popularized in a work of fiction: Dan Brown's *The Da Vinci Code*.

We dealt with the history of the canon in chapter 2. Through a gradual process of collecting books that were accepted by the universal church as inspired Scripture, a consensus on a definitive list was reached by the Fourth Century. But the canon had already taken a very familiar form by the end of the First Century, and the books were chosen not by political machination but by the application of four very appropriate criteria: Was the book written by an apostle or a close associate working under the umbrella of his apostolic authority? Was it accepted by all the apostolic churches? Did it proclaim the Gospel, the faith that was handed down from the original apostles? Did it impress itself on the church as coming with the power and conviction of the Holy Spirit? The canon did not leap fully armed from the head of Constantine like Pallas Athena from the head of Zeus in 325 AD. It was for all practical purposes already in place by the end of the First Century, though the process of building a *full* universal consensus took until the Fourth Century to be completed.

## THE CONSPIRACY THEORY

The conspiracy-theory version is much more exciting, especially if you are looking for an excuse to dismiss the testimony of the apostles to Jesus or an opportunity to impress ignorant people with your supposedly esoteric knowledge. We will lay out the version of it that Dan Brown used in his popular mystery novel *The Da Vinci Code*, and then look to see how it stands up to the actual historical evidence. The novel is a fast-paced page turner made fascinating by its use of many accurately described details of European art and architecture. The theory spun out of those details,

though, is more fictitious than the mystery story itself: that the Holy Grail is not the cup of Christ but the womb of Mary Magdalene, who was secretly the wife of Jesus. But that is a whole extra rabbit hole we don't need to go down right now. In order to set up that alternative timeline, Brown first has to poke holes in the standard canon of Scripture, because of course it does not tell the same story at all.

The critical conversation for our purposes occurs in chapter 55.[8] Harvard "symbologist" Robert Langdon and his companion Sophie visit Langdon's friend Sir Leigh Teabing seeking information to help them in their quest for the secret of the Holy Grail, hidden, as Langdon knows, in the paintings of Leonardo Da Vinci. To prepare Sophie for that revelation, Teabing first has to give her a different view of the authority of the Bible (which, after all, tells a slightly different story).

"Everything you need to know about the Bible," Teabing says, can be summed up in one sentence: "The Bible did not arrive by fax from heaven." In other words, "The Bible is a product of *man*, my dear, not of God." The way man created the Bible was that Jesus' life was recorded by "thousands" (!) of his followers, but then only a select few of those accounts were allowed to be read and the others were suppressed. "More than *eighty* gospels were considered for the New Testament, and yet only a relative few were chosen." That would be the four we know: Matthew, Mark, Luke, and John.

How did this choosing take place, and more importantly, why? "The Bible, as we know today, was collated by the pagan Roman emperor Constantine the Great." Wait, wasn't Constantine himself a Christian? "Hardly. He was a lifelong pagan who was baptized on his deathbed, too weak to protest." So why did he back Christianity as the new official religion if he wasn't a Christian himself? "Constantine was a very good businessman. . . . He simply backed the winning horse." And at the Council of Nicaea (AD 325), he transformed Christianity into a religion that could serve his purposes for unifying the empire by mixing it with the paganism Romans already believed in.

This transformation of the original Christian faith included voting on the deity of Christ—which apparently nobody had thought of before. "Until *that* moment in history, Jesus was viewed by his followers as a mortal prophet. . . . Jesus' establishment as 'the Son of God' was officially proposed and voted on by the Council of Nicaea." Why? It was all a power play to shore up the emperor and his cronies. "The early church

---

[8] Dan Brown, *The Da Vinci Code* (N.Y.: Anchor Books, 2003), pp. 249-56.

literally *stole* Jesus from His original followers, hijacking His human message, shrouding it in an impenetrable cloak of divinity, and using it to expand their own power."

The part of this alleged process that concerns us here was the supposed creation of the canon as a power play to insure the dominance of the approved political faction. "Constantine commissioned and financed a new Bible, which omitted those gospels that spoke of Christ's *human* traits and embellished those gospels that made Him godlike." Bottom line: "The modern Bible was compiled and edited by men who possessed a political agenda." Faithful testimony to the real historical Jesus had nothing to do with it. In fact, the real story was suppressed by sheer political power, and the Catholic Church has been engaged in a massive cover-up ever since.

## THE HISTORICAL REALITY

How does this alternative imaginary history stack up against the facts we actually know? To put it bluntly, there is hardly a word of truth in it. The alternative story is not created simply by choosing different facts to emphasize. It actually depends on outright fabrications of its own "facts" (or, to use a slightly less polite word, lies).

Were there thousands of people writing lives of Jesus? Certainly there were more than four, but no responsible scholar thinks there were "thousands" in any time period that is relevant. Were more than eighty gospels "considered" for inclusion in the New Testament? Considered by whom? Almost none of the other gospels was ever seriously considered for canonization at all, because they are too late to be viable candidates. The Council of Nicaea certainly did not start with any list of eighty-four gospels that was then narrowed down to four. That was not even on the agenda, which focused on the date of Easter and the attempt to find consensus on the nature of Christ as human and divine. Constantine certainly did not "collate" (i.e., collect together) the New Testament then, or have it done, because as we have seen, a canon almost identical to the one we have today was already functioning, accepted without controversy by churches across the Empire, more than two hundred years before the Council was ever called. He did commission fifty copies of the New Testament to be made, but that is hardly the same thing as "collating" an arbitrary version of it.

Even details not directly connected to the canon are highly questionable. Was Constantine a lifelong pagan and not a true Christian? Here are words from one of his own prayers, recorded by his contemporary, the church historian Eusebius: "Under thy guidance have I

devised and accomplished measures fraught with blessings; preceded by thy sacred sign I have led thy armies to victory." The sacred sign would be the cross of Christ, which Constantine had used as his banner ever since he saw a vision of the cross with the words "*In hoc signo vinces*, By this sign shalt thou conquer." So, the God to whom he is praying must be the Christian God. No other God was associated with that sign.

The prayer continues. "Therefore I have dedicated to thy service a soul duly attempered by love and fear. For thy name I truly love, while I regard with reverence that power of which thou hast given abundant proofs, to the confirmation and increase of my faith." As a result of this faith—what other faith than Christian faith can it be?—Constantine promises to rebuild churches destroyed in previous persecutions. "I hasten then to devote all my powers to the restoration of thy most holy dwelling place."[9] One can certainly question his understanding of Christian theology, but clearly this is a man who professes Christian faith. He has faith in the Christian God strong enough to motivate him to action. It is true that he was not baptized until his final illness, but this was a common practice among Christians at the time because they feared that sins committed after baptism might not be forgiven. That is not a clear understanding of the Gospel, but it hardly makes such people pagans rather than Christians.

Did the Council of Nicaea "vote" on the deity of Christ? In a sense, yes. It was called to deal with the Arian controversy, which had arisen because a theologian named Arius had denied the deity of Christ. He viewed Christ as a very exalted supernatural being, but a created being, not fully God. But even that fact reveals how distorted the conspiracy-theory version of the events is. Teabing gives the impression that Jesus was revered only as a purely human rabbi right up to that moment of time. "Until *that* moment in history, Jesus was viewed by his followers as a mortal prophet. . . . Jesus' establishment as 'the Son of God' was officially proposed and voted on by the Council of Nicaea." But nobody—literally *nobody*—at the Council of Nicaea thought of Jesus as only "a mortal prophet" and nothing more. They all believed that a powerful supernatural being had been incarnated in Jesus of Nazareth.

The question the Council debated was whether that being was the fully divine Son of God or something less. The purely human Jesus was not replaced by the divine Son of God at Nicaea for the simple reason that such a concept of Jesus never existed. One of the earliest documents in the New Testament, from about 51 AD, is First Thessalonians. Only twenty years

---

[9] Eusebius of Caesarea, "The Life of Constantine," *Nicene and Post-Nicene Fathers*, 2nd series, ed. Philip Schaaf (Peabody, MA: Hendrickson, 1995), 1:513.

after the crucifixion and resurrection of Jesus, Paul is already presenting Him as the divine "Son from Heaven" (1 Thes. 1:10). In his famous Pentecost Sermon, preached less than a couple of months after the resurrection, Peter speaks of Christ as one stronger than death who is exalted to the throne of God and capable of sending forth the divine Holy Spirit (Acts 2:24, 33). There is not one shred of evidence of any period of time at all when the followers of Jesus thought of him as a mere mortal man and nothing more. The *assumption* by conspiracy theorists that there "must" have been such a time is not evidence. In fact, the (First-Century) canonical Gospels are already full of passages that imply Jesus' deity, and some that directly claim it. "Before Abraham was born, I AM" (John 8:58) is perhaps the most impressive. "Before Abraham was born, I was" would have been a pretty bold claim, but what Jesus actually said not only claims pre-existence but uses a translation of the sacred Hebrew name of God, *Yahweh*, "I AM." If material like that did not go back to the beginning, it would have been being debated at Nicaea in the first place.

So, the bottom line for our question: Is it true that "Constantine commissioned and financed a new Bible, which omitted those gospels that spoke of Christ's *human* traits and embellished those gospels that made Him godlike"? The very opposite is true, which is evident to anyone who has read the canonical Gospels and compared them with the so-called apocryphal "gospels" of the Second Century and later. The four Gospels of the New Testament are full of the humanity of Jesus, presented right alongside His deity. (And there is no evidence of "embellishment" either, by the way. The claims to deity do not just show up in later manuscripts!) The Jesus in those Gospels got hungry and thirsty, He had to sleep—indeed, He got so tired on one occasion that He was sleeping right through a storm on the Sea of Galilee and had to be woken up to still the storm and calm the winds and the waves. That passage (Mark 4:35-41, cf. Mat. 8:23-27, Luke 8:22-25) is typical in that it has the very real humanity of Jesus and His equally real divine power right next to each other so we can experience the difficulty the disciples had at first in getting their heads around it. "What manner of man is this, that even the winds and the waves obey Him?"

By contrast, it is precisely the apocryphal "gospels" that downplay Jesus' humanity. They are full of what by contrast with the more sober New-Testament Gospels looks like pious fiction for the gullible: Jesus as a boy, for example, is making clay models of animals with his friends, and then Jesus throws his bird up into the air and it comes to life and flies away. The fact is that the humanity of Jesus is all over the canonical Gospels right alongside His deity, and the *merely* human Jesus does not appear in *any* gospel of any kind from the ancient world. Teabing's representation could not in fact be further from the truth.

So, again, bottom line: Was "the modern Bible . . . compiled and edited by men who possessed a political agenda"? Was that agenda to alter the original theology about Christ in order to solidify the power of Constantine, and was it done at the Council of Nicaea in 325 AD? In fact, Constantine's position as Emperor was already solid by that time. His calling the Council was evidence of the security of his power and influence in the Empire, not an attempt to create it. In fact, the Council of Nicaea simply recognized a canon that had already been coming together for a long time. In fact, its delegates used that canon to settle a theological controversy that existed, not because other gospels needed to be suppressed, but because the four canonical Gospels that they all accepted presented a picture of Jesus, going all the way back to the time of Jesus, that was hard to get your head around.

The picture was hard to get your head around because Jesus was hard to get your head around. How could the same Person be God and man at the same time? In fact, the deity of Christ was not "voted on" at Nicaea as a new "proposal." It was affirmed in clearer terms than ever before because it had been hanging over the church's attempts to understand what they were dealing with ever since the disciples started asking, "What manner of man *is* this?" In fact, the other "gospels" were not "suppressed" because they had an alternative view of how to answer that burning question that was being rejected for political reasons. They were not indeed "suppressed" at all. Nobody was ever jailed for copying or reading them! They were simply not approved for use in worship or for use in deciding doctrine. Why not? Because they were too late and spurious to be helpful in dealing with the question insistently posed by the original testimony as recorded in the original documents: "What manner of man *is* this?"[10]

## CONCLUSION

We started our discussion of the canon in chapter 2 by noting that the church was not ultimately based on a book. (Of course, in a sense it is based on a book, the Bible; but not in an ultimate sense.) It was *ultimately* based on a Person. The book, the documents that belong in the book, the criteria for discerning those documents that belong in the book, the manuscripts of those documents, the criteria for evaluating those manuscripts: All these things are important because the Person is important. They matter because the Person matters. The documents that belong in the

---

[10] For further information on the formation of the canon see chapter 2 of this book and also Paul Copan, *"How Do You Know You're not Wrong?" Responding to Objections that Leave Christian Speechless* (Grand Rapids: Baker, 2005), pp. 218-40.

Book and the words that belong in the documents are accepted because He accepted one group of those documents (the Old Testament) and commissioned the other (the New).

"You search the Scriptures," that Person said, "because you think that in them you have eternal life; it is these that speak about me" (John 5:39). All the evidence says that they speak authentically, truly, trustworthily, and well. And so they leave us with the very same question they first posed and then answered for the early church: "What manner of man *is* this?" The early church answered at Nicaea, "He is the Christ, the Son of the living God, incarnate in human flesh. He is fully God and fully man. He is the Lamb of God who taketh away the sin of the world."

How will you answer?

# CHAPTER 6

# "People used to believe in miracles because they didn't understand science. Don't we know better than that now?"

It is a common assumption that ignorance of science made it easy for primitive people to believe in miracles. Now that we know how nature actually works, some people think, we are no longer susceptible to such naïve beliefs. Ironically, it turns out that the really naïve and ignorant people are the ones who make that assumption. Three considerations make this irony apparent: Ancient people knew more than we give them credit for; what they knew was quite sufficient to prevent them from naively accepting a miracle out of ignorance; and the relationship of miracles to scientific laws may be more complicated than we think.

## ANCIENT IGNORANCE?

First, most modern people are actually pretty ignorant about how ignorant ancient people were—or weren't. I grew up thinking that people believed the earth was flat until Columbus proved them wrong by sailing West to reach the East in 1492. Everything about that thinking was incorrect. Columbus of course did not prove anything. He never reached the East because America was in the way. But even if his quest for the Indies had been successful, it would not have told educated people even in his own day anything they did not already know. We have known that the earth was a sphere at least since Eratosthenes (285-194 BC), who actually computed the circumference of the earth to within a few hundred miles of its accurate figure. And he was not the first person to figure this out.

You can actually observe the curvature of the earth for yourself by watching a ship sail away from the harbor or even a semi-truck approach from over the horizon in the Great Plains. The ship will not simply become smaller until it becomes too small to see. The ship or the truck will actually disappear from the bottom up (or appear from the top down) because it is dipping over beneath (or rising up above) the horizon as the earth's surface curves down away from you. The Greeks, the Egyptians, the Babylonians, and other ancient people were all certainly smart and observant enough to figure this out.

The difference between us and ancient people is that they had not yet *formalized* the scientific method: the cycle of observation, hypothesis, experiment, confirmation (or not) of the hypothesis, revision of the hypothesis, repeat. When we did so in the West in the Seventeenth Century, it gave a great boost to our ability to understand the laws of nature comprehensively, test our understanding of them rigorously, and see how they relate to one another systematically. But the ancients were neither ignorant nor unobservant nor incapable of critical thinking. They did not know as much science as we do, of course, but they knew quite enough to keep them from accepting miracles out of sheer ignorance and naivety.

## ANCIENT KNOWLEDGE

Take one of the most important miracles of the Christian faith, for example: the Virgin Birth (or more accurately, virginal conception) of Christ. Joseph, Mary's husband and Jesus' earthly step-father, did not accept the Virgin Birth due to any ignorance about childbearing at all. He would not have known the details of genetics and embryology that are available to us, but he knew perfectly well where babies come from, and he knew just as well that he had not been involved in producing the one that had showed up in Mary's womb. That is why he was planning to end their engagement.

It took a visit from an angel to convince Joseph that Mary had not been messing around with someone else. You can form your own judgment about whether he was right in coming to believe that a miracle had happened. But one thing is clear: His ignorance of scientific law had nothing to do with it. He knew the *relevant* facts about the birds and the bees as well as we do, and he made the same logical conclusion about what the evidence he was confronted with meant in the light of them that we would have made. You may or may not agree with his later decision to revise that conclusion, but you cannot dismiss it as the result of stupidity or ignorance on his part. The facts just do not support that interpretation.

All right, the reason Joseph accepted the miracle was not his ignorance of science. Maybe, then, he accepted it because of his knowledge of something else. That is a hypothesis that we cannot dismiss out of hand. (It would be very unscientific of us to do so!) No doubt Joseph would have said that his prior knowledge of Mary's character and his faith in the power of God both combined with the testimony of the angel to make believing in the Virgin Birth a logical conclusion. That combination of factors certainly made it a possible conclusion for him in a way that it is not for many modern people. But we have now eliminated the modern person's

knowledge of science and Joseph's supposed ignorance as the explanation of the difference.

So what is the explanation? Maybe the difference is not Joseph's ignorance of science but *our* ignorance of something else. What would that be? To answer that question, we must take a detour into the history of philosophy.

## MIRACLES AND SCIENCE

Modern skepticism about miracles has its ancestry in philosopher David Hume's work *An Enquiry Concerning Human Understanding* (1758), particularly chapter 10, "Of Miracles." Hume knew better than to try to prove that miracles are impossible. He knew you cannot prove a negative. But he tried to prove that it is never rational to believe in a miracle, and his effort proved very influential—though once we understand its flaws we will see that it is really quite unconvincing. Here's how his argument went.

1. A miracle is a violation of a natural law.
2. Natural laws area based on "uniform experience." (This is because science works by repeatable experiments, and until everybody who does the experiment right gets the same result, you have not formulated a natural law yet.)
3. Because a person reporting a miracle is (by definition) going against the whole testimony of "unalterable" human experience, it is always more likely that he is either deceived himself or is deceiving you than it is that he is telling the truth.
4. Therefore we are never rationally justified in believing that a miracle has happened.[11]

This argument might seem pretty convincing at first. Indeed, many people have been convinced by it. But there are at least two flaws in it that render it useless as a guide to evaluating the possibility of miracles.

The first flaw is the definition of a miracle as a violation of a natural law. If we do not accept that definition, then the whole rest of the argument becomes moot. And there is no good reason for Christians to accept it. We simply do not know how God works miracles. Does He invoke His higher authority to break the laws he set up for nature to operate by, or does He suspend them, or does He just apply a force to

---

[11] Daid Hume, "Of Miracles," *Eighteenth-Century English Literature*, ed. Geoffrey Tillotson, Paul Fussell, Jr., and Marshall Waingrow (N.Y.: Harcourt, Brace, & World, 1969), pp. 893-903.

nature that was not anticipated by our calculations in order to produce results we would not have predicted?

C. S. Lewis in *Miracles* gives the example of a pool table to illustrate that last possibility. The laws of physics say that if I shoot the que-ball into the eight-ball at such and such a velocity, from such and such a direction, with such and such spin, encountering it at such and such an angle at such and such a position on the table, the eight-ball will go into the side pocket. If on its way there somebody reaches his hand out and gives it a shove, so that it goes into the corner pocket instead, no laws of physics have been broken—not a single one. The hand being invisible (if it belongs to God) doesn't change a thing. The ball simply obeys those laws perfectly in the light of a force we had not anticipated when we set up the shot. That is why Lewis gave a very different definition of miracle: not a violation of natural law but rather an "interference" with the normal operations of nature "by a supernatural power."[12]

Note carefully: I am not claiming that God does not or cannot ever violate the laws of nature, which, after all, He set up. That is more than we know. But unless we know that He *does* violate them in order to work miracles (and we don't, because many of them can be easily explained on the other models), Hume's argument is moot. It never even gets off the ground.

What is the second flaw? O.K., even though we don't have to, let's grant just for the sake of argument that a miracle violates a natural law. Hume is still in trouble. He is guilty of circular reasoning, or "begging the question." How so? It is not in fact true that scientific laws are based on "uniform" or "unalterable" experience. The uniformity of human experience is simply not something that is available for scientific observation. Nobody has ever surveyed all the experiences of the human race on any point whatever—nor could we if we wanted to. Therefore, the "unalterability" of that experience is a metaphysical, not a scientific, claim. Unavoidably, then, scientific laws are actually based on *consistent* experience *as far as we know.* That is by definition the most that science can claim.

Here is a good way to see how Hume was cheating. What does the word "uniform" mean? It means that there have been no exceptions. But if we are trying to find out whether a particular miracle happened or not—say, the resurrection of Christ from the dead—then whether or not there has ever been an exception to our normal experience of what happens after

---

[12] C. S. Lewis, *Miracles: A Preliminary Study* (N.Y.: MacMillan, 1947), p. 10.

death is the very thing we are trying to find out. It is the very question we are asking. You cannot sneak your preferred answer ("no") in as evidence for itself at the beginning! Hume is basically saying, "No, there wasn't an exception there." Me: Why not? Hume: "Because there have never been any exceptions." Me: So, you're saying there are no exceptions because there are no exceptions? Hume: "Uh-oh, you caught me, lol."

The entire human race minus only one person is not "uniform." We are told that 500 people saw the risen Christ. Did they, or didn't they? Hume's argument is not a way of answering that question. It is a way of avoiding it while pretending to give an answer to it. To find out whether there was an exception or not, we have to go and look at the evidence, like we did in chapter one. And we should do it without a prior bias for either answer. Hume's argument is nothing more than a clever and sophisticated was of biasing the outcome. And you should not let him get away with it.[13]

## CONCLUSION

Bottom line: Science is not, by its very nature, capable of telling us whether or not miracles can happen. It might help in answering the question whether a particular one *has* happened, as with the before-and-after X-rays that showed the sudden and medically inexplicable disappearance, apparently in response to the prayers of our congregation, of a cancerous growth in a lady I once knew. Science, through the X-rays, provided relevant data used in the answer. But even then, the final answer depends on how we answer two other questions that simply will not fit into any test tube: Is there a Someone who is capable of interfering with the normal operations of nature? Is this particular example of such interference the kind of thing He would do?

Maybe the answers to those questions have something to do with what Joseph knew and modern people don't. That has a whole lot more to do with whether miracles have happened than anything we know and Joseph didn't. His supposed ignorance of science should simply be taken off the table as a factor in evaluating his beliefs. That much is certain.

---

[13] For further discussion of miracles and when we should believe in them, see Paul Copan, *When God Goes to Starbucks: A Guide to Everyday Apologetics* (Grand Rapids: Baker, 2008), pp. 53-66, and C. S. Lewis's classic work *Miracles: A Preliminary Study* (N.Y.: MacMillan, 1947).

# CHAPTER 7

# "That a man rose from the dead takes a lot of believing. How could you ever have enough evidence for a belief like that?"

This question is related to the so-called "extraordinary claims" argument: Extraordinary claims (like the resurrection of Christ from the dead) require extraordinary evidence—and however much evidence the believer presents, it is never going to be enough.

The argument does make a certain amount of sense. The more unusual a claim is, the more outside of normal experience it is, the more evidence most people will need before they believe it. And they are not wrong to feel that way. If you tell me that Tom Brady won the MVP award in the NFL, I might just take your word for it. If you make the same claim for a no-name rookie offensive lineman, I'll probably ask for some documentation.

What if I said to you, "Did you hear what happened in the funeral home last night? Some guy got up out of his coffin right in the middle of his funeral and walked away!" You would probably be skeptical, and rightly so. This is why even committed Christians who believe that God can and does perform miracles don't believe every urban legend they hear without good confirming evidence. There are too many fraudulent faith healers and credulous repeaters of gossip in the world, and, besides, if miracles were not rare, they wouldn't be miracles.

Non-believers are within their rights to demand good evidence before they accept a claim like the resurrection of Christ from the dead. But is it reasonable to set the bar for evidence so high that no possible array of proofs could ever clear it? There are actually some claims that would justify such a move. A claim that involved a logical contradiction would certainly qualify. If you tell me you have just drawn a square circle, I'm not even going to want to look at the figure before deciding that you are very much deceived. Why not? If you made your figure round, it won't be a square; if you gave it four corners, it won't be a circle. Calling it a square circle just abuses language. Like the square circle, all other genuine logical contradictions are also just incapable of being true, no matter how much "evidence" seems to support them.

Some non-Christians think that natural laws are so tightly woven into the fabric of reality that any miracle claim at all is on the same level as a square circle. But we already saw in chapter six that the very nature of the scientific observation on which such laws are based does not allow for such a blanket conclusion. David Hume might have been right if he had only said that it is often, or even usually, more likely that a person reporting a miracle is deceived or deceiving than it is that he is telling the truth. The frauds and the gossips have certainly managed to convince *me* of that much. The fatal flaw in his argument was his claim that it *always* is. That is more than his argument was capable of proving.

We agree then that we should demand *good* evidence for an extraordinary event like a miracle, but not evidence so extraordinary that it could never be found. This raises two crucial questions. First, how can we tell when the extraordinary claims argument is making an unreasonable demand? And second, what criteria need to be met for the evidence for an extraordinary event like the Resurrection of Christ to be adequate to justify informed assent?

## UNREASONABLE DEMANDS?

Here is a good tipoff for when the extraordinary claims argument is asking too much. The extraordinary claims argument should be rejected whenever the conclusion pointed to by the evidence can be denied only by making other claims just as extraordinary as the one in question.

The resurrection of Christ is a good example of this dilemma. Surely to claim that a man was raised from the dead is an extraordinary claim. I'm not going to believe it without some very good evidence. But supposing we don't make that extraordinary claim in the case of Jesus. What are we going to put in its place? We would have to pick from an array of counter-claims, none of which comes even close to being the least bit "ordinary." We would have to claim that five hundred people all had the same hallucination. Is that not an extraordinary claim? It is just as far outside the known psychological nature of hallucinations as the resurrection is outside the normal experience of what follows death. Or we could claim that ten out of eleven men were executed, and the eleventh was exiled, for what they knew to be a lie. Maybe that would not be absolutely impossible, but, yes, it would be pretty extraordinary.

The claims that have to be made to avoid accepting the resurrection get even more bizarre. We could claim that being beat to a bloody pulp, nailed to a cross, spending a day bleeding out and fighting asphyxiation, getting stabbed with a spear and showing clinical signs of death (the "water

and blood" that flowed out of Jesus' side), and being certified as dead by professional executioners left Jesus still alive and strong enough to let himself out of a sealed tomb. You see, He was only "mostly dead," and Miracle Max . . . Oh, never mind. Or we could claim that his body was still in the tomb but the Jewish officials who wanted desperately to squelch the infant Christian movement never bothered to go get it and nip the whole thing in the bud, which should have been very easy for them to do. Or maybe a passel of clueless wimps like the disciples were capable of stealing it (and that just throws us back to the problem of how they spent the rest of their lives).

Which extraordinary claim do you want to make, if you are not a believer? Pick your poison. The extraordinary claims argument simply does not help us to understand what happened in such a case. You cannot avoid extraordinary claims just by not believing, because *something* happened on the morning of the first day of the week in Jerusalem two thousand years ago—something unavoidably extraordinary. Not believing in one of those extraordinary claims simply means you are defaulting to one of the others.

So which extraordinary claim should we default to? Unless you know in advance that miracles are absolutely impossible, you have no legitimate reason for eliminating the resurrection and preferring one of the other extraordinary explanations on any basis that is not arbitrary. And we have shown in this chapter and the last one that you do not have, and cannot have, such knowledge. Science by its very nature is not capable of giving it to you. So claiming that the extraordinary claims argument lets you eliminate one of those extraordinary claims in favor of one of the others is simply mistaken. Of itself, it does no such thing. It is just a cover for your bias against supernatural explanations. Go ahead and be honest and admit your bias for what it is and stop claiming that you are only going by the evidence while Christians believe in fairy tales!

The extraordinary claims argument backfires for skeptics on many levels besides the specific question of the resurrection of Christ. If you simply refuse to accept the possibility of a miracle no matter what the evidence says, then you are committed to naturalism—Nature is all that there is. But then you have to believe that the universe just popped into existence out of nothing for no reason. Is that not an extraordinary claim? You have to believe that after doing so it proceeded to organize itself, without any outside help, into DNA and life, and that by random chance a creature evolved whose mind can perceive and understand the (mental) mathematical laws by which the (purely physical) natural world operates. You have to believe this by blind faith, despite the abundant evidence that matter plus energy plus time plus chance is utterly incapable of producing

on its own the kind of specified, complex order required for life to function. Is that not an extraordinary claim?

We see then that the extraordinary claims argument ends up telling us nothing about what is true or even what can be true. It takes our common-sense realization that important claims require good evidence and absolutizes it. It turns it into a tyrant that excludes possible explanations on what look like rational grounds, but which turn out to be arbitrary. It therefore should just be dropped.

## CRITERIA FOR REASONABLE EVIDENCE

We are now ready for the second question: What criteria need to be met for the evidence for an extraordinary event like the Resurrection of Christ to be adequate to justify informed assent? Solid evidence is a must, of course, but by itself it might still leave us scratching our heads and wondering which extraordinary claim to prefer. We can answer that question by returning to two questions we posed at the end of the last chapter: Is there a Someone who is capable of interfering with the normal operations of nature? Is this particular example of such interference the kind of thing He would do?

My belief in the resurrection of Christ then is a cord woven from three strands. First is an acceptance of at least the theoretical possibility of the existence of the God of Abraham, Isaac, and Jacob. His existence for me is confirmed by the resurrection and by many other arguments that make His existence the best explanation for the existence and form of the universe. But all that is required at the outset of examining the evidence for the resurrection is a willingness to entertain His action as a possibility. The second strand is the historical evidence we laid out in chapter one. And the third is the appropriateness of this act to His character as revealed in the Exodus, in prophecy, and in the Person of His Son.

As we said in chapter one, the final reason why the case for the resurrection is so convincing is that we are talking about *Jesus*. This is not some random dude in some miscellaneous place that we are saying rose from the dead. This is a man whose coming had been prepared by Providence and predicted by prophecy for two thousand years, whose friends kept asking themselves, "What manner of man *is* this?" (Luke 8:25) and being compelled to answer that question in theistic terms. This is the reassertion of a life that had already shown itself to be sovereign over life and death. If ever there was a man about whom we could believe such a thing, it is this man: It is Jesus of Nazareth.

The resurrection then is not just a weird happening. It is the high point of God's testimony to the human race about Jesus. It begins in the prophets who predicted His coming, rises to a climax in the Gospels which narrate it, and continues in the Epistles which explain it: "This is my beloved Son, in whom I am well pleased. Listen to Him!" (Mat. 3:17). The resurrection is the keystone of that testimony. It seals and nails down the truth about who Jesus was: "Thou art the Christ, the Son of the living God" (Mat. 16:16). It is the ultimate vindication of Jesus' own claim that "I and the Father are one" (John 10:30). It assures us that Jesus was indeed nothing less than what He claimed to be: God manifested in human flesh. It seals the redemption God had promised from the day Adam fell and had worked toward throughout the Old Testament. It keeps the promises that the Father had made to Abraham and that Jesus had made to His disciples. It fits as the climax to the whole history that stretches from Eden to the present moment. It is the exclamation mark that belongs at the end of *that* sentence, the icing that belongs on *that* cake.[14]

## CONCLUSION

A God who *could* do it; strong evidence that He *did* do it; the conviction that He *would* do it: Take away any of those strands and we have only a tantalizing possibility. Weave them all together and add the power of that resurrection to give new spiritual life even now by faith, and we have precisely the extraordinary confirmation that such an extraordinary event requires. I commend it to you as the power of God for salvation for those who believe.

---

[14] For further discussion of miracles and when we should believe in them, see Paul Copan, *When God Goes to Starbucks: A Guide to Everyday Apologetics* (Grand Rapids: Baker, 2008), pp. 53-66, and C. S. Lewis's classic work *Miracles: A Preliminary Study* (N.Y.: MacMillan, 1947).

# CHAPTER 8

# "Science has proved that human beings evolved over millions of years rather than being created in six days. Why are you still clinging to ancient myths?"

A superficial understanding of both science and Scripture can certainly create the impression that they offer completely opposed accounts of the creation of the universe and the origins of mankind. The person asking this question thinks that they are so opposed that you can only believe the Bible by rejecting science, which is not a viable option for modern people who do not have their heads in the sand. For such a person, science wins and Christianity loses—period, end of story.

If you have followed me through chapters 6 and 7, you probably realize already that the reality of the relationship between science and the Bible is, shall we say, more complicated than that. When we stick to what science has *proved* (as opposed to what a lot of scientists believe as part of the current reigning mega-theory), it turns out that the essence of the biblical creation story is actually upheld by science, and none of it is necessarily overturned.[15]

## SCIENTIFIC PROOF?

What has science proved? In the first place, we have to realize that the word *proved* has a different connotation in science than it does in logic or mathematics. To understand the proof of the Pythagorean Theorem is to understand that it is necessarily true and not open to revision. There is never going to be a right triangle the square of whose hypotenuse is not equal to the sum of the squares of the two sides. But *all* scientific conclusions

[15] If you can only read one book on the question of origins and the Bible, I recommend Francis A. Schaeffer, *Genesis in Space and Time: The Flow of Biblical History* (Downers Grove, IL: InterVarsity Press, 1972). Other important works include Philip E. Johnson, *Darwin on Trial* (Downers Grove, Il.: InterVarsity Press, 1993) and the works in the bibliography by William A. Dembski, Michael J. Behe, Edgar Andrews, and Hugh Ross.

are by definition open to revision, because science primarily depends on inductive rather than deductive reasoning.

Some of science's conclusions are pretty solid. I'm not holding my breath over whether the sun is in the center of the solar system. I lose no sleep over the possibility of a revival of geocentrism. But even the most solid scientific statements can get tweaked in surprising and unexpected ways as further information becomes available. Newton's laws were once thought to be as solid as anything ever gets, and of course they still work well when applied on a small scale. But Einstein's theory of relativity revealed that they were not as ultimate as we thought, and on a cosmic scale the curvature of space had to be taken into account. Now advances in quantum theory, string theory, and indeterminacy suggest that even Einstein may not have had the last word.

Given that understanding of scientific "proof," many people would be surprised to learn that pretty solid understandings coming out of physics actually are consistent with the biblical account in astonishing ways. Science for example has proved that the universe is not eternal. It was not always there (as in the once-popular "steady state" theory) but came into existence basically out of nothing at a definite point in the finite past known as the "Big Bang." Does the Big Bang correspond to the moment in Genesis when God said, "Let there be light"? It is certainly a tantalizing possibility. Indeed, physicist Robert Jastrow has described the history of thought this way: For many long years the scientists scratched and clawed their way up the mountain of knowledge. And when they finally pulled themselves up onto the peak, they found the theologians sitting there waiting for them.[16] Bottom line: "The essential elements of the astronomical and biblical accounts of Genesis are the same: the chain of events leading to man commenced suddenly and sharply at a definite moment in time, in a flash of light and energy."[17]

There still remain two pretty huge apparent areas of disagreement between Genesis and the standard scientific account of creation. Did life evolve by chance, or was it created? And did this happen over millions of years or in six literal twenty-four hour days, only a few thousand years ago? When we pay closer attention to what science has actually *proved* and to what the biblical text actually *says*, the conclusion is that there is no ultimate

---

[16] Robert Jastrow, *God and the Astronomers* (NY: Warner Books, 1980), pp. 105-6.

[17] Ibid., pp. 3-4.

conflict between biblical *teaching* (as opposed to interpretation) and scientific *fact* (as opposed to theory) at all.

## EVOLUTION OR SPECIAL CREATION?

Did life evolve by purely random chance, or was it created by God? What science has proved is that there is a process called natural selection that causes organisms to adapt to their environment. Random mutations—changes—happen in genes from time to time. Most of them are harmful or trivial, but occasionally one occurs that happens to give the organism a leg up in the quest for survival. Those advantageously altered genes get passed on at a higher rate to the next generation because it is much easier to reproduce if you survive than it is if you don't. Over time this causes the gene pool of the species to be different. The new gene replaces the old one in the population, and the better-adapted species hangs around to be studied by future biologists.

Imagine a limited environment—say, a college campus. The college installs high-speed ceiling fans with razor-sharp titanium blades exactly five and a half feet above the floor in each room. Tall people all eventually get decapitated because they do not remember to duck every time they pass through the room. Now, it's kind of hard to get married and have children after having your head chopped off. Pretty soon, therefore, only people with genes for short stature are reproducing. The population gets shorter, not just because tall individuals have been eliminated by the environment, but because their genes have been weeded out of the population. Eventually, only people with genes for shortness are born. The gene pool of that population adjusts. This is the famous "survival of the fittest." (Fitness must be understood in terms of a specific environment, as in this fictional college where height is a disadvantage.) And it actually works. It is why we get nasty super viruses and resistant bacteria from attacking their populations with antibiotics if we aren't careful.

That is what science has proved. It should be non-controversial. It accounts for a lot of changes within a species, including Darwin's famous finch beaks. But what biologists have done is to *extrapolate* this process to try to make it explain *everything* about the origin and history of biological life. It certainly explains a lot of observed changes within a species. That it can produce a whole new species is not so obvious. That it can produce life from non-life ("abiogenesis") is not proved at all. In fact, it is virtually impossible.

Life, you see, is based on DNA, and DNA has all the characteristics of a *code*. What are the characteristics of a code?

If you are walking on the beach and see sand dollars arranged to form the English sentence "Beware of shark," nobody thinks the shells just happened to wash up in that form due to random wave action. Why not? Ocean waves do not know English letters, English spelling, English vocabulary, or English grammar. But whoever arranged those sand dollars had to know all four of those complex patterns to create the sentence. They are independent of each other, and they are very specific. There is nothing about the shape of the letter B to connect it with the sound of a B (the voiced bilabial stop). There is nothing about that sound to connect it with the combination of certain specific other sounds to signify the concept of "beware," of watching out for some danger. And there is nothing about those shapes or those sounds or those words to tell you to put them in the order that has the object of the preposition after the preposition. To write that message, every single sand dollar making up every single letter representing every single sound in every single position to create every single word in every single position to create the grammatical sentence—all of that has to be just right. This is called "specified complexity." What are the odds of that happening by chance?

For any one letter of that sequence to have been washed up randomly by chance would require almost impossible odds. For all fifteen of them (including the spaces) to have done so in the right order to satisfy the independent demands of phonics, spelling, vocabulary, and grammar, simultaneously, by pure chance, is beyond impossible. Nobody thinks it happened that way. The most secular and atheistic evolutionist on the planet if he is walking on that beach thinks, if he is honest, that some intelligent agent wrote that sentence for a purpose—either to warn us of shark activity or just to mess with our minds.

Well, DNA is like that. It has "specified complexity," just like our sand-dollar sentence. And there is no evidence—none—of specified complexity of that kind ever having been produced by random chance. Nature is capable of creating certain kinds of order without outside help—think of a crystal, for example. Specified complexity is not one of those kinds of order. Evolution is just not capable of creating life from non-life. An intelligent Creator is required to get that process started. Otherwise there would be nothing to evolve. Naturalistic evolutionists are just in denial about the inability of their theory to get life started. They want to believe it explains *everything*; but it cannot.[18]

---

[18] For the classic explanation of specified complexity in DNA and why it could not have happened naturally, see Francis S. Collins, *The Language of God: A Scientist Presents Evidence for Belief* (N.Y.: Free Press, 2006). Collins was head of the Human Genome Project. Collins

Now, the text of Genesis is interesting in the light of these facts. It uses a technical word—Hebrew *bara'*—which means to create out of nothing. It is only used for an act of creation that cannot be accounted for by previously existing materials or situations. And it also uses other words for create that could mean to mold or work with existing material, words that also appear in the creation story. But *bara'* is used at three very crucial points: the initial creation of the universe (the Big Bang?), the creation of conscious life, and the creation of man. How much did God use evolution (natural selection) to produce the complexity of the current biosphere? Christians themselves give different answers to that question, ranging from very little to an awful lot. But what the text of Scripture proclaims is that there was a supernatural act in at least three very crucial moments—and those moments are exactly where science tells us they needed to be. If we limit ourselves to what science has proved and do not confuse it with what some scientists have extrapolated despite the actual scientific facts, the Bible and science are actually in remarkable agreement.

## THE TIME FRAME

The other big issue where people see a conflict between science and the Bible is the age of the earth. The red shift (a Doppler effect happening to light because the stars are traveling away from us due to the expansion of the universe after the Big Bang) tells us that the universe is several billion years old, and geology and the fossil record seem to indicate a very long history of life on the planet. For example, if the universe were only a few thousand years old, the light we can see from a great many stars and galaxies should not have reached us yet. Yet Genesis seems to speak of the whole process of creation as having been finished in six days, and its genealogies seem to put the creation of human beings only six thousand years ago.

Bible-believing Christians are themselves divided over how to handle this question. Young-Earth Creationism (YEC) takes the Genesis account literally and has to explain why the earth looks so old when it is really not. It has to suggest wild surmises: that the speed of light has not remained constant since the beginning, or that God created a young earth with the "appearance" of great age. Old-Earth Creationism (OEC) accepts the scientific evidence for the age of the universe and has various ways of

---

accepts theistic evolution and rejects Intelligent Design in terms that are not fair to it, two positions I reject. But he clearly shows and well explains the impossibility of DNA having come about by purely chance processes. Another good explanation that avoids these problems is British scientist and Christian Edgar Andrews, *Who Made God: Searching for a Theory of Everything* (Grand Rapids: Evangelical Press, 2009), esp. pp. 177-213.

reconciling that conclusion with the biblical account. They include taking the first six "days" of Genesis as symbolic of long eons or ages of time (the "Day-Age Theory"), positing a large period of time between Genesis 1:1 and 1:2 (the "Gap Theory"), or suggesting that the days are a literary device to organize the creation story and have nothing to do with dating at all (the "Framework Hypothesis").

All of these solutions have problems. YEC theorists seem dismissive of the strength of the case for an old earth, and worse, often do not seem to understand how science works. YEC apologists will typically find some fact of geology or paleontology that can be interpreted as consistent with a young earth and bring it out with a spirit of "See, I told you so! *Ergo, QED*!" OEC scientists on the other hand tend to argue from *correlations* of many threads of evidence from many fields: astrophysics (the red shift), geology, ice core samples, tree rings, carbon dating, etc. They are looking for where these very different types of measurements point in the same direction. This argument from correlation is a much stronger type of argument, and the only one that has a chance of convincing real practicing scientists who are not already committed to a dogmatic YEC view. Also, a creation that looks old when it is not seems to many to put God in the position of being deceptive in general revelation.

None of the OEC positions, on the other hand, succeed in perfectly explaining all the details of the biblical text or making them perfectly square with the apparent history of life on earth. Nobody would see the alleged "gap" between Genesis 1:1 and 1:2 who was not looking for a way to reconcile Genesis with an old earth. It might be there, but the text does not indicate it—nor does any other text of Scripture. The ages represented by the six days do not perfectly correspond to the ages posited by science. And while the Framework Hypothesis is attractive, there is nothing in the text to mark a transition from the six days to the straight chronological history that follows them. Also, OEC proponents have to explain how there was animal death before the Fall, when Genesis seems to imply that the curse incurred by Adam after his disobedience was the source of death in a previously perfect creation.

Is the OEC view even possible biblically? YEC advocates argue that it is not. They insist that every time the Hebrew word *yom* ("day") is used *with a number* in the rest of the Old Testament, it refers to a literal 24-hour day. But it certainly can be used for a longer period, just as the English word day can. And there are problems with taking it as literal even with the numbers in Genesis 1. The sun was not even created (or revealed) until day four. So whatever the "evening and morning" were on the first three days, they were not *literal*. They could not be, without a literal sunrise and

sunset to mark them. So, the OEC position is left open as an option by the biblical text. It is not heresy, as YEC proponents often try to argue.

## CONCLUSION

Which view is correct? I have an opinion, but I am not even going to give it, because defending that view is not my purpose here. There are two much more important points than that to take away from this discussion. First, *every* view of the age of the earth has problems. Make no mistake. You have to decide which set of problems you want to live with, and you need to be charitable toward those who favor a different view. Dogmatism is not justified here. Christians often make defending the biblical view more difficult than it needs to be by overreaching. We can afford a little humility.

The second point is the most important. Every Christian view of the age of the earth has problems, but naturalistic evolution has an even bigger problem—a fatal problem. As we saw above, it cannot even get the process or creation started without God, and its extrapolation of natural selection into a theory of the *origin of life* is a non-starter. It offers a method of producing the specified complexity required for life that is utterly incapable of performing that function in any time frame recognized by science.

I do not need to know how perfectly to harmonize the Bible with science to know that the biblical account of creation is true. It has answers to ultimate origins, the origin of life, and the origin of man that evolution cannot provide, and without which we cannot understand who we are. How much did God use the process of natural selection in the story of the development of life after its creation? Some. A more specific answer than that I am not in a position to give, and neither are you. But we do not have to know the answer to that question to know that in the beginning God created the heavens and the earth and created Adam and Eve in His own image. Of that we can be sure. And with that we must be content.

Christian Publishing House will offer what it understands to be the length of the creation days with biblically sound articles.

**Short Article**

DID GOD CREATE THE EARTH IN SIX 24-HOUR DAYS?

(http://bit.ly/2y0fzyZ)

**Long Article**

GENESIS 1:1 BDC: IS THE EARTH ONLY 6,000 TO 10,000 YEARS OLD? ARE THE CREATIVE DAYS LITERALLY, ONLY 24 HOURS LONG?

(http://bit.ly/2XSYjeH)

# CHAPTER 9

# "Just because the Bible is true for you, why does that make it true for me?"

That is a very good question. To answer it, we have to think for a moment about what we mean by truth, and what makes a truth true "for" someone.

## TRUTH ABOUT TRUTH

Truth is a property of propositions, or statements, such that their content corresponds to what they claim is so. If I say it is raining, and little drops of water are falling from a cloud and whacking me in the head, the statement is true because it says those drops of water are falling, and they are. If I say the same thing in the middle of a drought on a bright, sunny day without a cloud in the sky, the statement is false because it says those little drops of water are falling, and they are not.

There are some truths that are rightly understood as true "for me" or "for you," and they can be very different. If I say, "Vanilla is the best flavor of ice cream," that statement is true for me if in fact vanilla is my favorite flavor, but it could be false for you if you like chocolate better. This kind of truth is called *subjective* truth, because it is true for the subject who says it, and that is all. It is really a statement about me as much as it is a statement about ice cream. I get to decide whether it is true (for me) or not, and you don't need to agree. A very different statement can be true for you.

Other truths are true for everybody whether they agree with them or not. An object in motion tends to remain in motion; an object at rest tends to remain at rest. That is why in an emergency stop of your car, your body pushes into the seatbelt/shoulder strap uncomfortably and might smash into the dashboard if you didn't have your seatbelt on. Your body, being a body, wants to remain in motion in obedience to the laws of physics. If you don't like vanilla, you are allowed to disagree with me about the best ice cream, and for you, chocolate is the best. But if you don't like physics, your body is going to lean into that shoulder strap anyway. It won't care two cents about your opinion. This is an example of an *objective* truth,

that is, a truth that is true for everybody whether they believe it, or like it, or not.

## IDENTIFYING OBJECTIVE TRUTHS

Now, pretty much everybody can see that both kinds of truth exist. The difficulty comes in trying to agree about which kind we are dealing with in a given case. We started here with two pretty plain examples. Hardly anyone thinks that Newton's laws are mere subjective opinions, and only a boor would try to turn his opinion about the best ice cream flavor into a universal absolute binding on everyone. The mischief is that there is a huge territory in between those two points where the classification is not clear at all to a lot of modern people.

Take for example a statement like "Murder is wrong." Is that true for everyone no matter what they think about it, or is it just something we believe because of how we were brought up? Would it be true for us, but maybe not for a cannibal raised in a stone-age tribe? Or would it be true for most people, but maybe not for the son of a Sicilian Mafia family? For most of history, people in the West thought the wrongness of murder just as solidly objective a truth as Newton's laws of motion. If you didn't see it, there was something wrong with you. Lots of people today would hesitate to say so and wonder, maybe somewhat uncomfortably, whether they shouldn't accept one of the more subjective versions above. Who are we, after all, to judge the Cannibal or the Mafiosi? After all, everything is relative.

If your first impulse was to cut the Cannibal or the Mafiosi some slack because after all everything is relative, welcome to the modern world. I hope, though, that you are honest enough to be at least a little uncomfortable with that impulse. You should be uncomfortable with it, for two reasons. First is the nagging realization that you might have just let someone get away with murder. And second is the logical problem that "Everything is relative" is one of those claims that simply cannot be true. If *everything* is relative, then the statement that everything is relative is only relatively true—which means that some things are not relative. Relativism is self-refuting. Buy we've been taught that *judging* is wrong. (Always? Absolutely? What if you are judging somebody for judging? Oh, wait . . .). That can't be right. But that is the way most of us feel today. How did we get ourselves into such a conflicted mess?

## THE ATTACK ON OBJECTIVITY

We are, ironically, the victims of our own success in the search for truth. The Seventeenth Century saw the rise of modern science. The rigorous application of the scientific method began to open up the secrets of nature in ways that were truly impressive: the heliocentric solar system, the physics of planetary motion, the existence of microorganisms, the circulation of the blood, all of this leading to an understanding of nature as a *system* of rational laws expressible in mathematics—and the list goes on. In natural science there was a way that disputes could be settled: repeatable experiments that anyone could duplicate. A host of previously held beliefs about the natural world and how it works were being exploded and replaced by new understandings that seemed to have, well, a scientific basis. The impression was created that objective truth and science were simply one and the same, and that any belief that could not be put into a test tube was mere subjective opinion.

By the Eighteenth Century, philosophers were lining up to try to explain why science seemed to work so well. This effort gave us the English Empiricists, who believed that all knowledge comes through the senses. (David Hume, whose view of miracles we discussed in chapter 6, was one of those guys.) So what does that say about knowledge of non-physical realities like values or like right and wrong? That kind of knowledge seemed harder to justify on an objective basis.

Then in the Twentieth Century the view of skeptical empiricists like Hume was updated and called "Logical Positivism." Logical Positivists wanted to get philosophy away from useless speculation and focus it on truths they thought could actually be known. To that end, they introduced what they called "The Verification Principle": The meaning of any statement is found by specifying the set of (physical) conditions that would serve to verify or falsify that statement. The Verification Principle a useful tool as far as it goes. We used it when we decided above that "It is raining" was true because we were getting whacked in the head by drops of water. But here's the problem: If you cannot specify such conditions, the Positivists said, your statement is not a real statement at all, even though the grammar of the sentence in which you expressed it made it look like one. It is a "pseudo-statement." It is not false; it doesn't even rise to that level. It is actually meaningless as a statement about objective reality. So, by this view, "Murder is wrong" looks like an objective statement about murder, but it's really a subjective statement about the speaker's feelings. It reduces to "I don't like murder."

By the Twentieth Century then, many intellectuals had concluded that we can only make objective truth claims about science, and everything else, which includes all statements about meaning, purpose, value, right, or wrong, is only subjective truth. This was called "Modernism." "Murder is wrong" was the same kind of statement as "I prefer chocolate"—except that it had stiffer consequences and a lot more people agreed with it. But in principle, it was no different.

This thinking seeped down into popular culture, and that is why you might have been uncomfortable saying that "Murder is wrong" is objectively true—true for everybody. Now in the Twenty-First Century, the reigning philosophy is so-called "Post-Modernism." It thinks it has gotten over Modernism and seen through its errors, but it has just made the relativism of late Modernism only worse. Rather than restoring faith in truth claims about purpose and value, many Post-Modernists no longer have confidence that even scientific statements can be objectively true. It might be better if instead of talking about Post-Modernism we called it what it really is: Hyper-Modernism!

## RECOVERING OBJECTIVITY

OK, I've explained how we got into the conflicted mess we found ourselves in above, unable to justify our opposition to murder on any objective basis, unable to judge the tribal person who commits murder, and forced to contradict ourselves in order to avoid doing that judging. How do we get out of it? We have to realize that the fact that they create this dilemma tells us that Modernism and Post-Modernism cannot be right. There have to be at least some non-scientific truths that are objectively true, true for everybody whether they like it or not. Murder is wrong (if we define murder carefully as the unjustified taking of innocent human life) is one of them, and we *know* that it is, even if we cannot explain precisely how we know. (I will try to deal with that question later.) So we realize that we can no longer automatically lump all truth claims into the "I like chocolate" category as our default setting without even thinking about it.

## OBJECTIVITY AND THE BIBLE

If we have made that realization, we are ready to get back to our original question: "Just because the Bible is true for you, why does that make it true for me?" The Bible would be true for both of us if the truths it communicates are objective truths. It need not be true for both of us if they are subjective truths. Well, what kind of truths are they?

A lot of the statements the Bible makes have to be taken as objective. They may be true or false, but either way, they are true or false, *period*—not just for one person and not another. They include factual claims: Jesus rose from the dead. Well, He either did, or He didn't. He is either still dead, or He isn't. We can disagree about that, but if we do, one of us is wrong. His body won't be missing from the tomb when I look but suddenly appear there, like Schroedinger's cat, when you do. There is not a separate "truth" about something like that which can be one thing for me and another for you, any more than you can put the brakes on in your car without dealing with Newton's laws. There are also a lot of "murder is wrong" type statements, and we have to face at least the possibility that they could be objectively true (or false) as well.[19]

## CONCLUSION

We must conclude then that the person who asks, "Just because the Bible is true for you, why does that make it true for me?" is asking the wrong question. The right question, the one we should be asking, is "Does the God that the Bible presents to us exist?" If the answer is yes, then the Bible's message is true whether we believe it, or like it, or not, and we have to decide how we are going to deal with that situation. If the answer is no, then the Bible is an ancient book full of probably many truths and many errors, and you can take or leave them as you like.

So how can we know whether the God who is the Father of Jesus Christ exists? There are many lines of evidence that I think point together to that conclusion. One of the most important is the resurrection of Christ from the dead, which has come up more than once already in this book. Here is one more that is brought up by the discussion in this chapter. We find that however hard we try, we cannot escape the existence of objective truths, and that among them are basic ethical principles like "Murder is wrong." What does this mean? It raises an interesting question.

How could such objective truths exist, and how we could know that they exist, if the universe is just an impersonal collection of atoms happening by chance? Atoms aren't true or false about each other; they just

---

[19] For further discussion of how some truths can be objective and universal, see Paul Copan, *"That's Just Your Interrpetation": Responding to Skeptics Who Challenge your Faith* (Grand Rapids: Baker, 2001), pp. 25-40, C. S. Lewis, The Abolition of Man ((N.Y.: MacMillan, 1947), and Douglas Groothuis, *Truth Decay* (Downers Grove, Il.: Intervarsity Press, 2000).

are. This is a difficult problem. Objective truths exist, and people can know them. That should not be true in a naturalistic universe. But if God exists, and if He created the world, and if *He* thinks murder is wrong, then that would explain why that proposition is true at all places and times and for all people in the universe that He made. And if He made human beings in His image, then that would explain how we are able to truly perceive the universal validity of those ideas.

Christianity turns out to be a hypothesis that explains this feature of the real world better than any other explanation.[20] That is certainly suggestive. Of course, if Jesus did *not* rise from the dead, it remains a nice theory and nothing more. But the fact that it solves an otherwise intractable problem gives us one more reason to pay very good attention to the evidence for the resurrection as it comes up in chapters 1, 6, and 7.

If the Bible is just true for me, or for you, who cares? But if it is *true* . . .

---

[20] If you are interested in more discussion of the ways the biblical world view has better explanatory power than its rivals, see Francis A. Schaeffer's follow up to *The God Who is There* (Downers Grove, Il.: InterVarsity Press, 1968), *He is There and He is not Silent* (Wheaton: Tyndale House, 1972).

# CHAPTER 10

# "How can you base your modern life on a book that was written for a primitive culture?"

The world we live in is certainly very different from the world that existed in Bible times. How is it different? It has a more formalized understanding of the scientific method and enjoys the knowledge and the practical applications that flow from it. Those practical applications are called *technology*. As a result of that technology, much of the world has better sanitation, better nutrition, better health, better health care when it doesn't have better health, more spacious and comfortable dwellings, and much more efficient means of transportation and communication than our ancestors could ever have dreamed of. As a result of all of that, most of our lives are longer, safer, and less painful than most of theirs were. At the same time, we also have more powerful weapons and, if we are not careful, a more powerfully negative impact on the environment than they could have imagined. Still, we are in many ways better off. Few of us would seriously want to go back to having a life span of less than forty years.

## SECULARIZATION

All that technology tends to make us think about the world differently from the way our ancestors did. Inventions such as the electric light, the internal combustion engine, and the personal computer (and now, putting the personal computer inside the smart phone) have fundamentally altered the way in which we experience the world. Most of us have had less direct interaction with nature for about a hundred years, and now less direct interaction with each other. (I have watched my students texting each other while sitting at the same table instead of looking up from their phones and having a face-to-face conversation.) Instead of interacting with nature and each other, we are now surrounded by machines. We live in a world dominated by machines. This affects how we experience the world in multiple ways.

One of those ways is the pace of change. Change has speeded up as technology advances, and we experience change differently. Our ancestors used basically the same horse-and-buggy technology, with only minor and

relatively trivial improvements, for over two thousand years. Then we got the steam locomotive only a couple of centuries ago. And think what happened in just the Twentieth Century. My father could remember seeing his first automobile and his first airplane, and he lived to see men travel to the moon. Almost all the radical changes to transportation of the last two millennia happened in one lifetime!

There are other areas in which change has accelerated in ways that are astonishing. Electronic media is certainly one of them. I myself can personally remember my first color television. I can remember typing term papers on a manual typewriter. I can remember when a computer filled a room and only major corporations and governments could afford to own one. Many of my readers on the other hand will have no memory of a world without email, texting, word processing, and the internet—maybe no memory of a world without taking those conveniences for granted. But the printed book had lasted five hundred years basically unchanged before that.

These realities—an environment dominated by machines and an unprecedented pace of radical change—have created a new way of experiencing of the world. We call it *secularization*. The way modern people experience the world makes it easier for them to think about the world in secular terms, even though the world itself (apart from our increasingly artificial ways of living in it) has not changed at all. Why do we call this phenomenon secularization? The word *secular* is from a Latin word meaning age, i.e., a period of time; so "secular" thinking treats the world as if only time existed, ignoring eternity. In other words, it treats the world as if only this world exists, not the next—as if only matter exists, not spirit. Ironically, the more distant *this* world is from our experience of it, the more we are alienated from the spiritual world as well.

How does this impact on our thinking work? In technology, change is in your face and it is almost always for the better. Would you rather have a new SUV or a gas-hogging clunker from the 1970s? Would you rather have the latest smart phone or a TRS-80? So your default setting is that change is going to happen, it is always going to happen, it is going to happen rapidly, and it is going to be good; the new is automatically going to be better than the old. You probably just assume that this is always true and fundamentally true because it has been true so often in your experience. This unthinking assumption encouraged by our experience of modern life is why we have heard politicians promoting "change" as if it were automatically a good thing without specifying what change exactly they were pushing! Secularization makes people susceptible to such nonsense. Well, here is one more question: Does *all* change *really* work

that way? Does Nature change in the same way that technology does? Does the world?

Because the technological kind of change, the way machines improve as a result of human creativity, dominates our environment, it makes it harder for us to believe in permanent things, things that don't change. It sets us up to be victims of what C. S. Lewis called "chronological snobbery," the assumption that the newer is always better and that contemporary ideas are automatically cool and with it and older ones automatically outmoded.[21] And because human beings did all this cool stuff, it is easier than it used to be to assume that we really don't need God any more. (Nobody asks where those humans got their capacity for creativity and innovation or the raw materials they use to create that innovation.) Not only Nature, but also the Supernatural, may therefore seem more distant to many people.

## THINGS THAT DO NOT CHANGE

But stop and think for a moment. Secularization may have changed the way we tend to experience the world, but has it really changed *the world*? No. Clearly not. Nature keeps right on working the same way it did for the ancient Romans. Milk still comes from cows, even if kids in the inner city have lost that connection and just think it comes from cartons. The natural laws we use to make cars and planes and computers work, that make the planets orbit the sun, that enable your body to turn food into cells and energy, are exactly the same as they have always been. They are exactly the same as they were before we figured out how to manipulate them on the level that we do now.

All right, then. Some things have changed, and some things have not. And the things that have changed have more to do with how we tend to experience reality than they do with the nature of reality itself. Two conclusions follow from this realization. First, it is very possible that an ancient book could still have important things to say to us, especially if it is talking about the things that have not changed and do not change. Second, we might need to listen to those ancient voices more than ever, because they will be more in touch with precisely those unchanging facts about the world that we are most apt to miss because we have covered them over with the machine world we have made in our own image.

---

[21] See C. S. Lewis, *Surprised by Joy: The Shape of my Early* Life (N.Y.: Harcourt, Brace, and World, 1955), pp. 107-8.

Let's think about an example. In chapter 9 we used "Murder is wrong" as an example of a statement that was not scientific but was nonetheless objectively true. We suggested it got its objective and universal truth from the fact that God thinks murder is wrong, which makes it true for everybody who exists in the universe that God made, in every place in the universe that God made, and at every moment that transpires in the universe that God made. OK, what has changed and what has not with reference to murder? In a primitive society I could kill my neighbor with, say, a club, an arrow, a knife, or a spear. Now I can still do those things, but I have a number of additional options: I could shoot him with a handgun, I could run him over with a car, I could tie him to a railroad track, I could blow him up with dynamite, or I could throw him out of the window of a skyscraper. None of these options were available to the primitive tribesman. But they are only methods. The meaning of the act, the wrongness of the act, and, if it is wrong, the reasons why it is wrong—none of that has changed at all. If you think the proliferation of methods has changed the meaning, the wrongness, or the rationale of the act of murder, you are just horribly confused.

## THE BIBLE AND THE PERMANENT THINGS

The Bible (and other ancient literature too) is about the things that have not changed and do not change. The people told about in those books pursued the same goals we do: power, wealth, and pleasure, or meaning, purpose, and love. The fact that they used different methods to pursue those ends does not really change anything. If the Bible is what Christians believe it is, the Word of God, then it is a message from the very One whose thinking makes objective and universal truths objective and universal. He tells us that murder is wrong ("You shall not murder," Exodus 20:13) and, just as importantly, He tells us why: because human beings were made in His image and are therefore immensely valuable, because their lives are His property and not ours to destroy, and because He loves them and we should too (Gen. 1:26-8, John 3:16, etc.). Neither Siri nor Alexa can give you that same message with the same authority, nor can they really add anything significant to it.

The Bible was written *in* cultures that are in some ways more primitive than ours, but it was written *for* human beings. It was written for human beings in whatever culture and time they find themselves. And it was done in a simpler time perhaps so it could better cut through the hectic clutter of the modern world to get us back to the basics. Precisely because its human writers were not distracted by our confusing proliferation of ever-changing

methods, it is able to speak, to the very heart of our humanity, of the things that do not change.

Other ancient literature can do this as well: *The Iliad* can show you the futility of war driven by human pride. *The Odyssey* can show you the power of faithful love. *Oedipus* can show you the mystery of how character and destiny interact. *The Aeneid* can show you the nobility of sacrifice in a noble cause (and, without intending to, the tragedy of making an idol of that cause). They do this with a depth that has kept them alive for more than two millennia because those values do not change. They carry in their lines a wealth of pondered human experience without which we would be sorely impoverished.

The Bible does all of that and adds to it the authority not just of great human creators but of the great Creator of the whole world. Like Homer, Sophocles, and Virgil, biblical writers such as Moses, David, Isaiah, and Paul were great men who had experienced life intensely and thought about it deeply, in ways that reflect its pathos, its mystery, its beauty, its tragedy, and its goodness. If we were right in chapter 1, they added to all of that a wisdom greater than any mortal can find merely on his own, a wisdom that comes from above. It guaranteed that they would say exactly what we needed to hear, with no mixture of error. Alright, then. He who has ears to hear, let him hear.

## CONCLUSION

The word *primitive* doesn't just mean undeveloped; it can also mean original and unspoiled. In that sense, we need the Bible as a guide to our modern life precisely *because* it was primitive. It can root you in reality as no other book, ancient or modern—the reality that does not change.

# CHAPTER 11

# "Doesn't the Bible support genocide?"

So far, one feature of the Bible that has come out in our discussion is the fact that it confirms our moral instinct that the statement "Murder is wrong" is an objective, universal truth. So how could the same book support genocide, the attempt to wipe out of an entire race or people?

The impression that the Bible supports genocide comes from one incident: the conquest of Canaan by Joshua after the children of Israel were delivered from bondage in Egypt during the Exodus. There Joshua was given some instructions by God that understandably raise a lot of modern eyebrows. We had better look at the full reality of them without blinking and then see if we can provide some context to help us understand it all.

## THE CANAANITES

It starts with God speaking to Moses at Mount Sinai. After giving the Ten Commandments, followed up by a number of case laws about how to apply them, God helps Moses anticipate the conquest of Canaan, the Promised Land. Obviously after four hundred years of captivity in Egypt, the Israelites would find other people already living in the land they were being brought to—a land which had been promised to their ancestor Abraham but which they had never possessed as anything but aliens and strangers.

God promises to completely destroy the current inhabitants, the Amorites, Hittites, Perizzites, Canaanites, Hivites, and Jebusites. The Israelites are not actually commanded here to annihilate them; they are only responsible to destroy their places of worship lest they be tempted to idolatry themselves. "I will deliver them into your hand, and you will drive them out before you. You shall make no covenant with them or with their gods. They shall not live in your land, because they will make you sin against me; for if you serve their gods, it will certainly be a snare to you" (Ex. 23:31-33). These instructions are essentially repeated in Leviticus 33:50-55. The emphasis is not on slaughter but expulsion and the complete destruction of idols, temples, and other religious sites.

It gets worse, though. In Deuteronomy, Moses is preparing the people for their invasion of Canaan on the verge of entering the land. He reminds

them that when they were attacked on their way there by the Amorite kings Og and Sihon, they had "utterly destroyed" the "men, women, and children of every city" (Deut. 3:6). Then they are warned that when they enter the land they are to "utterly destroy" its inhabitants too, make no covenant with them, and not intermarry with them, but destroy all their religious sites "for you are a holy people to the Lord your God" (Deut. 7:1-6). In the cities they are not to "leave alive anything that breathes" (Deut. 20:16). In all these passages great stress is laid on the danger of the Israelites being corrupted by the idolatry and other religious practices of these people. The idea is that making a clean sweep is the only way to avoid such compromise and corruption.

Moses then dies right before the invasion, and the new leader Joshua is careful to carry out these instructions. At least ten times between Joshua 6:11 and 11:20, battles are mentioned in which Joshua "utterly destroyed" the enemy or "left no survivor." Yet in spite of all of this, the Canaanites were not in fact annihilated. At the end of his life, Joshua exhorts Israel to finish the job and not to intermarry with the survivors, lest God not continue to drive them out and they "become a snare" with the result that *Israel* in turn will perish from the land (Josh. 23:12-13).

## THE CONTEXT

The first thing to note is that it is not quite accurate to say that the Old Testament "supports" genocide. It does not "support" it; it *commands* it on one, and only one, specific occasion, the conquest of Canaan after the Exodus. The general teaching of the Old Testament about life and about warfare does not support genocide as a general ethical practice in any way, shape, or form. The one time when it was commanded still requires some explanation. But it requires it precisely because it was an *exception* to what we are normally led to expect from God and from His people. It was never the rule.

What was the rule? If you look at the general ethical principles laid down in the Old Testament, you would never get the idea that genocide could be a thing for Israel. The general tendency is to place *limits* on retaliation against one's enemies. The infamous *lex talionis* itself ("an eye for an eye and a tooth for a tooth," Ex. 21:24, cf. Lev. 24:17-21) actually had as its original purpose the limitation of what one could exact as punishment for injury: no more than the injury one had received. There are other provisions that put limits on the use of force even when it is legitimate. If a thief is caught in the act of breaking in to your house and struck so that he dies, there is no guilt for his blood. But if the sun has risen, there is (Ex. 22:2-3). In other words, you can defend your property, with

deadly force if necessary—but you can't hunt the thief down and kill him later, rather than turning him over to the law, which will require ,not his life, but restitution as punishment.

Indeed, personal vengeance is forbidden altogether. It belongs to God (Deut. 32:35) and is prohibited to men. "Do not say, 'I will repay evil'" (Prvb. 20:22). "Do not say, 'Thus I shall do to him as he has done to me'" (Prvb. 24:29). Jesus' command in the New Testament that we should actually *love* our enemies (Mat. 5:44) was not completely new. It was already anticipated in Proverbs 25:21. "If your enemy is hungry, give him food to eat; and if he is thirsty, give him water to drink." The idea of being good to your enemies is reiterated in no uncertain terms. If your enemy's donkey wanders away, you return it. If it falls under its load, you release it and help it up (Ex. 23:4-5).

These laws so far apply to personal conduct. What was the general teaching of the Old Testament about the ethics of warfare? It is covered in Deuteronomy chapter 20. The teaching on warfare is consistent with the personal ethics we have seen so far. What we find is a concept of limited war which was far more enlightened than that of the nations surrounding Israel at the time, and in which genocide is explicitly forbidden and even bloodshed is minimized. When approaching a city to besiege it, the Israeli army was first required to offer it terms of peace. This was not a choice; it was a policy. Israel could only attack it if the terms were refused. When they defeated the city, only the men (i.e., the combatants) were to be struck with the sword. Women and children were specifically to be spared. This was the general rule, but an exception was made once and once only: for the cities in Canaan during the conquest. There Israel should not "leave alive anything that breathes" (Deut. 20: 16), lest again they be seduced into idolatry and the "detestable" practices that went along with it.

Once again, we see that in general the Old Testament not only does not support genocide, it explicitly forbids it. We are left, though, with the one glaring exception where genocide was commanded in explicit terms and inconsistently carried out. Why did God in that instance command something that seems so inconsistent with everything else He had said? That is the question we have to try to answer.

## THE RATIONALE

A twofold answer to that question is given consistently by the Old-Testament Scriptures, and the two parts of the answer are related. First, the wickedness of the people specially targeted had reached such a level that nothing less than complete destruction would suffice as a response, and

second, that wickedness had to be completely purged lest it prove a snare to the Israelites. Israel was after all a people newly separated from and still highly vulnerable to the temptation to mimic the idolatry that surrounded them as the default setting for ancient near-eastern religion. We must examine each part of that answer to see if it stands up. But one thing is clear at the outset: The Canaanite "genocide" was a special case, a one-off, unique situation that was never approved as a general policy or ever intended to be repeated.

That genocide was judgment for exceptional wickedness is stated clearly and forthrightly. When God was explaining to Abraham that his descendants would not actually possess the promised land until they had spent 400 years in slavery, the reason He gave was that "the iniquity of the Amorite is not yet complete" (Gen. 15:16). Then on the verge of this promise's fulfillment, Moses warns the people,

> Don not say in your heart when the LORD your God has driven them out before you, "Because of my righteousness the LORD has brought me in to possess this land," but it is because of the wickedness of these nations that the LORD is dispossessing them before you. It is not for your righteousness or for the uprightness of your heart that you are going to possess the land, but it is because of the wickedness of these nations that the LORD your God is driving them out before you, in order to confirm the oath which the LORD swore to your fathers, to Abraham, Isaac, and Jacob. (Deut. 9:4-5)

Can we imagine even the theoretical possibility that evil could become so pervasive and so deeply rooted in a given people and their culture that nothing less than razing it to the ground and starting over from scratch would be justified? I cannot imagine that I would ever be in a position to make such a call. But I cannot rule out the possibility that God could be in that position. In fact, if we accept the history that the Old Testament presents us, the Canaanites were not the first time He had done so. The Genesis Flood constitutes such a judgment on the whole human race, Noah's family only excepted. That case is perhaps easier to accept than that of the Canaanites because human beings in obedience to God were not involved in carrying out the sentence. Still, if God was justified in pronouncing that kind of judgment in the first case, there is no reason to deny Him the same prerogative in the second.

We have in our own generation been given a unique opportunity to appreciate the possibility of such a harsh sentence against a people and their

culture actually being appropriate. The brutality of ISIS[22] against those it deems the enemies of Islam reached a level of savagery that we have not seen since the Nazis and that we would not have been able to believe if the evidence for it had not been so inescapable. People were burned alive, crucified, and drowned, and these acts videoed and boasted about. I recall watching a video that showed ISIS mothers egging on their small children to celebrate and rejoice in such brutal torture and murder of innocent people taking place right in front of them—and they were receiving that lesson with enthusiasm. Where would you start trying to reform a people who had sunk so low and whose evil was so pervasive throughout their whole social structure?

Do not misunderstand me! I am not advocating or calling for such a response to ISIS or anyone else. Only God is in a position to make that call. No living human being has that kind of authority. I only offer ISIS as an example that can help us *imagine* a situation in which a full destruction, including women and children, might be justified. I offer ISIS as an example that can help us imagine how a complete obliteration of a culture so vile and corrupt that nothing can be salvaged from it might be justified. Human beings are indeed capable of creating a society that ingrown and that mired in its pollution, cruelty, and degradation. They do not often do it. But sometimes they do—and we have watched them do it. Thus our own recent history makes it easier to imagine and accept the hard truth that the Canaanites in Joshua's day might have been just such a people.

The sentence God had pronounced against the Canaanites was only inconsistently carried out. And Israel indeed suffered for its failure to complete the mission. The Israelites flirted with idolatry for the rest of their national existence. They absorbed the corrupt practices of their neighbors such as Moloch worship (which involved sacrificing one's firstborn by burning him alive), and finally had to be sent into exile and see the destruction of their monarchy over their failure adequately to repent of such atrocities.

Their story involves some harsh realities. But it does not involve anything that would compromise our view of their God's love or His justice—not unless we just refuse to believe in the realities that all of human history, including our own recent history, rubs our noses in. The fact is that the nations God judged were given opportunities for repentance, and those individuals who chose to trust Him were spared—like Rahab's family during the conquest and the Ninevites later. Far from being to blame for human

---

[22] THE GUIDE TO ANSWERING ISLAM: What Every Christian Needs to Know About Islam and the Rise of Radical Islam by Daniel Janosik (978-1-949586-76-3)

wickedness by commanding genocide, God shows Himself committed to dealing with it in ways that involve both justice and mercy, even when that mercy is as costly to Him as the Cross.[23]

## CONCLUSION

It is clear then that, contrary to the claims of cynical skeptics, the Bible does not support genocide. Its personal ethic and its ethic of warfare in fact rule it out as an available option for human beings trying to deal with the evil in the world. But the Bible does record at least two occasions on which the evil in the heart of man reached such proportions that God determined that a complete destruction of a society was the only appropriate response to it. The Bible is not cruel because it reports those occasions, but realistic in that it deals with them. And while it is full of such sobering justice, it is even more full of mercy and of hope. For it offers to us the complete pardon and forgiveness of our own sins given freely in response to faith in Christ, who underwent the destruction we deserve to pay for them. That is where the arc of the biblical narrative leads. Praise the Lord!

---

[23] For further discussion of these issues, see Paul Copan, *"That's Just Your Interpretation": Responding to Skeptics who Challenge your Faith* (Grand Rapids: Baker, 20010, pp. 161-70, and *When God Goes to Starbucks: A Guide to Everyday Apologetics* (Grand Rapids: Baker, 2008), 136-61.

# CHAPTER 12

## "Doesn't the Bible support racism?"

Racism is a charged term these days because of our own historical struggles to achieve racial justice. Negro chattel slavery in the United States was ended only by the tragedy of the American Civil War. But the slaves were freed with no adequate plan for helping them transition to full citizenship, and the oppression of the Southern states during Reconstruction combined with that failure to encourage a set of social attitudes and practices, centered in segregation, that relegated African-Americans to second-class status legally for generations. This situation was not redressed until the Civil-Rights movement of the 1960s succeeded in abolishing segregation and making equal rights and equal access the law of the land. Attitudes take longer to change than laws, and so we still wrestle with how to deal with the aftermath of that history.

It did not help that some Christians used the Bible to justify slavery. Their case had enough of a surface plausibility to make it convincing to large numbers of white Southerners. The Old Testament permitted slavery and the New Testament did not abolish it; moreover, the curse of Ham by Noah was taken to apply to modern Africans. This case was bogus, as we will see in the next chapter. But here we need to note simply that enough people believed it to make the claim that the Bible supports racism also believable to certain people. This chapter will show that, however believable that claim might seem to some, it is false.

We had better define racism. Racism as I will use the term is the sin of treating another human being differently—whether better or worse—because of external characteristics like the color of his skin or the shape of his features. It is the precise opposite of Martin Luther King, Jr.'s, dream of a day when his children would be judged not by the color of their skin but by the content of their character. Merely to state the alternatives so clearly and eloquently as he did is to see that one of those ways of judging people is wrong and inappropriate and the other is just and right. That is why racial prejudice is wrong: It is precisely *pre-judging* someone on a basis that is simply irrelevant to his status and dignity as a human being and as an individual. Character as lived out is a proper basis of judgment; skin color is not.

How then did anyone ever get the idea that the Bible is a racist book? It's not hard to see how a surface analysis could lead to that conclusion. Central to the whole Old-Testament story is God choosing one particular people, and not others, to be His own and to have a special relationship with Him. That could certainly look like racial favoritism. But when we look deeper, we find out that it was anything but. That deeper look starts now.

## THE CALL OF ABRAHAM

The Old Testament rolls out the story of the plan God set in action to respond to the fall of the human race into sin when Adam and Eve disobeyed Him in the Garden of Eden. Adam and Eve lost their immortality and their direct relationship with God and became subject to the curse as a result of their sin. But God immediately promised that the "Seed of the Woman" would someday crush Satan's head—the first hint of coming redemption (Gen. 3:15). He replaced their inadequate fig leaves with garments of animal hide and banished them from the Garden to make their way in the world and learn from bitter experience the consequences of their disobedience. But God continued to relate to them through grace, unmerited favor, as they worshiped Him through sacrifice and began to "call upon the name of the Lord" (Gen. 4:26). Even when their escalating sinfulness earned the judgment of the Flood, God did not abandon them, but preserved the race through the salvation of Noah and his family in the ark. Then came the moment that would give shape to the rest of the Old-Testament: the Call of Abraham.

Let's watch this event happening and then try to see what it means. Seemingly out of the blue, God appears to an apparently random man named Abram and says to him,

> Go forth from your country and from your relatives and from your father's house to the land which I will show you; and I will make you a great nation, and I will bless you and make your name great; and so you will be a blessing; and I will bless those who bless you, and the one who curses you I will curse, and in you all the families of the earth will be blessed. (Gen. 12:1-3)

The rest of the Old Testament is the story of this man's family and how the promise of blessing was kept for his descendants and expanded to include the promise that through them would come the Messiah, the Savior, whom we meet in the New Testament as Jesus of Nazareth.

What was God up to? What was His purpose in focusing on one family which grew into one special people and nation? Nobody helps us understand the strategy behind God's strange act better than C. S. Lewis:

> He selected one particular people and spent several centuries hammering into their heads the sort of God He was—that there was only one of Him and that He cared about right conduct. Those people were the Jews, and the Old Testament gives an account of the hammering process. Then comes the real shock. Among these Jews there suddenly turns up a man who goes about talking as if He was God. He claims to forgive sins. He says He has always existed.[24]

That man of course was Jesus. And the New Testament is the story of His coming to save, not just the Jews, but the world.

## A STRATEGIC CHOICE

There is a pattern to God's dealing with men throughout history: He works through an individual or a small group to reach a larger group. You see it in Jesus, who ministered to the masses but concentrated His attention on the twelve Disciples. Starting with that small group of men, He reached the whole Roman world with the Gospel in just one generation. That concentrated attention on a few paid off in a bigger impact on the many than could have been achieved by dividing His efforts among the whole population. We who follow those Disciples are told to maintain the same approach. Paul exhorted his disciple Timothy that "The things which you have heard from me" he should entrust to other "faithful men who will be able to teach others also" (2 Tim. 2:2). We focus on the few for the sake of the many.

God was doing the same thing in the Old Testament. There is what theologians call "general revelation," which comes through nature and conscience generally to all people. No one is neglected, but general revelation must by its very nature be less pointed and specific than "special revelation," which is directed to a more concentrated audience through the actual Word of God—orally for Abraham, in the Bible for us. Abraham and his descendants were singled out for special attention so that one people would have a fuller understanding of God's message which it could then share with the rest of the human race.

---

[24] C. S. Lewis, *Mere Christianity* (NY: MacMillan, 1943), p. 54.

Our minds were so messed up by the fall that we needed a lot of "hammering" to beat into our heads what God is really like. It was a process that lasted two millennia. The process had two purposes: to give Abraham and his descendants a sharper message that could be shared with other peoples, and to ready one people so that when Christ came He would come into a prepared context where the significance of His coming could be understood. The sacrificial system, the Exodus from Egypt with its Passover, and many prophecies over those two millennia gave meaning to the words of John the Baptist when it was time for them to be uttered: "Behold the Lamb of God who taketh away the sins of the world" (John 1:29).

As the recipients of this special revelation, the Jews received a great blessing and a great privilege, but also a great burden and responsibility: to share that blessing with "all the families of the earth" (Gen. 12:3). Unfortunately, many of them focused on the blessing and ignored the responsibility. They came to think of themselves as a special race and of the Gentiles—those poor uncircumcised barbarians—as inferior and unclean. In the First Century, a pious Jew would not enter a Gentile's house or even eat at the same table with him. In other words, those Jews through the human perversity they share with all races abused their privilege and their calling and became racist. That does not mean that God approved of racism or that the Bible supports it. In fact, as we shall see, the very opposite is the case.

## THE BIBLE AND RACISM

There are at least four ways in which the Bible shows itself to be a profoundly *anti*-racist book. In the first place, the very calling of the Jews as the Chosen People was given in terms that make it clear that their calling was precisely for the sake of all the other peoples. The whole point of calling Abraham and promising to make him a great nation and bless him is given in the climactic phrase that ends the call: "In you all the families of the earth will be blessed" (Gen. 12:1-3). We could call that phrase "the Great Commission of the Old Testament." Solomon got it. At his dedication of the Temple he prays this:

> Also concerning the foreigner who is not of your people Israel, when he comes from a far country (for they will hear of your great name and your mighty hand and your outstretched arm); when he comes and prays toward this house, hear in heaven your dwelling place, and od according to all for which the foreigner calls to You, in order that all the people of the earth

> may know Your name to fear You, as do your people Israel. (1 Kings 8:41-43)

Most of Israel forgot this emphasis. But after the Resurrection and the coming of the Holy Spirit, the New-Testament church took it to the next level, not just inviting the nations in but going *out* to them, to all of them no matter their race, to the very ends of the earth.

Second, it is stressed to Israel that their calling does not make them better than other nations because it was not based on anything about them that was superior to other peoples. As they were preparing to enter the Promised Land after their years of wilderness wandering, Moses warned them not to misunderstand what is happening:

> Do not say in your heart when the Lord your God has driven them out before you, "Because of my righteousness the Lord has brought me into possess this land," but it is because of the wickedness of these nations that the Lord is dispossessing them before you. . . . Know, then, it is not because of your righteousness that the Lord is giving you this good land to possess, for you are a stubborn people. (Deut. 9:-4-6)

It was not Israel's merit but God's grace that was the cause of their blessing. "The Lord did not set His love on you nor choose you because you were more in number than any of the peoples, for you were the fewest of all peoples, but because the Lord loved you and kept the oath which He swore to your fathers" (Deut. 7:7-8). Whether from Egypt or from sin, salvation in both Testaments is by God's grace alone and not by human merit (Eph. 2:8-10). There is no basis in the calling of Abraham for any feeling of racial superiority; in fact, it is quite the opposite.

Third, Israel is clearly condemned for her contempt for the Gentiles and lack of concern for their salvation. That is the whole message of the book of Jonah. The wayward prophet tries to get out of preaching to Nineveh, and when that effort is thwarted by the great fish, he does it with a bad grace and is upset when the Ninevites repent and are spared God's judgment. He is severely rebuked for his racist attitude: "Should I not have compassion on Nineveh, the great city in which there are more than 120,000 persons who do not know the difference between their right and left hand, as well as many animals?" (Jonah 4:11). God is concerned for the salvation of all peoples, but His prophet from the chosen people, instead of gladly fulfilling the purpose for which they were chosen, resents it. Sadly the rebuke he received did not prevent his attitude from becoming fully enculturated in Judaism by the time of Christ.

Finally, the New Testament brings to fruition the true purpose of the Abrahamic covenant, putting God's love and concern for all peoples front and center. The unity of the human race is explicitly affirmed. God "made from one man every nation of mankind to live on all the face of the earth" (Acts 17:26). Jesus' followers are commissioned to "make disciples of all the nations" (Mat. 28:19). In doing that, despite the racist prejudices of the early Jewish Christians of the Pharisaic party, the Gentiles are to be accepted on an equal basis. They need not be circumcised and become Jews to be Christians because when the first Gentiles were converted "God made no distinction between us and them" (Acts 15:9). Peter is rebuked for reverting to prejudice and refusing table fellowship to Gentiles (Gal. 1:11). One of the effects of the death of Christ is the destruction of the "middle wall of partition" that had separated cultural Judaism from other races (Eph. 2:14). No follower of Jesus can consistently remain a racist because the Gospel has revealed Gentiles as "fellow members of the Body and fellow partakers of the promise" (Eph. 3:6). Jesus died for people of "every tongue, tribe, and nation" (Rev. 5:9). All who have put their faith in Him must view each other and treat each other as brothers and sisters in Him.

## CONCLUSION

People whom God chooses are chosen are chosen for the sake of others. They are not chosen for any merit they possess. They are rebuked for acting as if they thought they were. Not only is there no basis for racism anywhere in Scripture, but the Gospel in the New Testament gives it what ought to be its final death blow. In the light of all of the above, it is hard to understand how anyone who has actually read the Bible could think of it as a racist book. Those who make that accusation have some agenda other than listening to what it actually says.

# CHAPTER 13

# "Doesn't the Bible support slavery?"

Because of the kind of race-based slavery that is part of our history, racism and slavery are inseparable issues for us as Americans. If the Bible is as deadly to racism as we saw in chapter 12, how could anyone possibly think it condones slavery? Well, at first glance it appears that the Old Testament permitted it, the New Testament tolerated it, and neither explicitly condemns it. Indeed, far from running a First-Century underground railroad, the Apostle Paul sent the newly converted runaway slave Onesimus back to his master (Philemon). After what we saw in the last chapter, it is understandable that someone might wonder, "What's up with that?"

My answer is that the Bible opposes slavery, but in a more subtle way than you might have expected. To understand how and why we need to know a few things about the biblical writers' position in history and then look at some principles they taught that did not come to full fruition for many hundreds of years.

## PRELIMINARY CONSIDERATIONS

First, we need to understand that, while slavery existed in the ancient world and was an evil, it was a very different thing indeed from the American Negro Slavery that mars our own history. In the first place, slavery in the ancient world was not based on race. One path into slavery was being taken as a prisoner of war. Another was being sold to pay off your debts. Race as such had nothing to do with it. Slavery that is based on race is much worse because the color of your skin creates a presumption of servitude that makes it much more difficult to regain your freedom or to be accepted as a free person again if you do. Paths out of slavery in the ancient world were more numerous and fluid than in the antebellum South. Your family or friends might save up their money and buy your freedom back, especially if you were a debt slave. Some slaves even were able to make a little money on the side and eventually purchase their own freedom back themselves. There were several categories of servitude, some more tolerable than others. (Being sent to the mines was a fate worse than

death.) Some forms of slavery were closer to what we would call indentured servitude.[25]

Still, slavery was not a desirable condition. Paul, in the midst of saying that Christians should remain in that status, slave or free, that they had before their conversion, allows that one who has the opportunity to win his freedom should take advantage of it, and warns that one who is free should not become enslaved to men (1 Cor. 7:21-4). Freedom is recognized as a good and slavery as a misfortune, but there are worse things than being a slave—like bringing the Gospel into disrepute by rebelling or failing to provide good service. The Apostle realizes that for most people in his time, slavery is simply a given, a fact of life that most of them cannot do anything about. Rather than trying to change the social order, he is more interested in teaching people how to honor Christ within it.

To us, used to living in a participatory democracy where we as citizens are expected to have an influence on public policy, that approach seems like a copout. But we have to understand that trying to change the social order of the Roman Empire by any kind of direct action was simply not an option that was open to New-Testament Christians. If they had tried, they would only have gotten a lot of people killed and made life more difficult for the slaves who survived. This does not of course mean that we should not take advantage of our opportunity to be a voice for justice. Our ancestors in the faith William Wilberforce and John Newton used their influence to get slavery itself and the slave trade abolished in England in the Eighteenth Century, and they are still role models for us to this day.[26] (Our own equivalent and parallel issue may be abortion, which also arbitrarily classifies a segment of the human family as less than fully human.) But Christians in the Roman Empire had to take a different approach. So let's see what the New-Testament writers taught about slavery and how they undermined that institution in the long run in ways that made Wilberforce not only possible but inevitable.

---

25 For more information see Keith R Bradley, "Slavery," *The Oxford Companion to Classical Civilization*, ed. Simon Hornblower and Antony Spawforth (Oxford: Oxford University Press, 1998): 670-73.

26 For a quick introduction to Newton and Wilberforce, see David Lyle Jeffrey, ed., *A Burning and a Shining Light: English Spirituality in the Age of Wesley* (Grand Rapids: Eerdmans, 1987), Jeffrey gives a rich anthology of the writings of the leaders of the First Great Awakening, with excellent introductions and notes.

## NEW-TESTAMENT TEACHING ON SLAVERY

Most of the direct teaching on slavery comes from the Apostle Paul. As we have seen, he accepted the existence of slavery as a fact of ancient life, no doubt a result of the Fall, but simply a given that Christians had to deal with. He has a lot to say about how Christian slaves and masters should approach the roles that society has given them.

The first point he makes is that being slave or free is not the most important fact about a person. Like whether you are a man or a woman, or whether you are a Jew or a Greek, it pales into insignificance next to being a child of God and a disciple of Jesus Christ (Gal. 3:28). Indeed, the slave is Christ's freedman and the free man is Christ's slave (1 Cor. 7:22). Paul's favorite self-designations are that he is the Apostle, the prisoner, and the *slave* of Jesus Christ. As a person in relation to the Roman Empire he is a free citizen with rights that he expects to be respected (Acts 16:37, 22:25). But in relation to God, he is the slave of Jesus Christ.

Christian slaves then are no different from Paul. They are both slaves of Jesus. Those who are also slaves in society serve Jesus by serving their human masters. They are to give them obedience and faithful service that comes from the heart because how they serve reflects on Jesus (Eph. 6:5, Col. 3:22, 1 Tim. 6:1). If their masters are fellow Christians, they have the additional motive that they are serving a beloved brother in Christ. Masters, on the other hand, are to be gentle, not ruling by threats, treating their slaves with justice and fairness, and recognizing them as Christian brothers (Eph, 6:9, Col. 4:1, Philemon 1:16). Slaves who have the opportunity to gain their freedom should take it, but something is vastly more important than whether one is slave or free, and that is whether our lives aid or hinder the spread of the Gospel. You treat your master or your slave well so that "the name of God and our doctrine will not be spoken against" (1 Tim. 6:1). How your actions affect your testimony for Christ matters infinitely more than whether they are personally advantageous for you.

## THE TEACHING AND ITS TRAJECTORY

It is understandable that a modern person might think that all this just reinforces an evil institution. But Paul is not supporting slavery. He is not pro-slavery; he is pro-love and pro-Gospel. And the way in which he supports *those* values actually undermines slavery in the long run far more profoundly than any attempted rebellion or slave revolt would have done. It does so in a couple of interesting ways.

First, Paul's commitment to love and the Gospel is premised on the profound equality of all men before God. Slaves and masters who are Christians are brothers in Christ. Their different social status in Roman culture is left behind at the church door. The master is Christ's slave, and the slave is Christ's freedman. All of us, in other words, by having Christ as our absolute sovereign, our Lord and Master, are His *bondservants*, owing Him complete and unquestioned obedience. And all of us as his slaves are set *free*—free from from the penalty of the Law, from the guilt and the bonds of sin. All true Christians simultaneously inhabit the identity of Christ's slave and that of his friend. In Christ, so far as a person's worth and spiritual standing are concerned, there is neither Jew nor Greek, man nor woman, bond nor free. Aristotle infamously based Greek slavery on the idea that some people are slaves by nature—that is, inferior. To be a Christian is to have that foundation for slavery stripped completely out from under you.

Second, the relationship Paul expects Philemon to have with his returned slave Onesimus on the basis of that equality makes slavery as men have known it virtually impossible for Christians (Philemon 1:10-20). In sending the runaway slave Onesimus back to Philemon, Paul is sending not just a slave but his own child in the Lord. Because Philemon is Paul's fellow Christian, he expects him to forgive Onesimus for having run away and be good to him now that he is back, not under compulsion but out of Christian love that flows from his heart. Onesimus is more than a slave now—he is a beloved brother. They may be master and slave to society, but *in* Christ they are brothers and *to* Christ they are fellow servants, on the same level.

Now, think about who is saying this. It is a man who calls himself the slave of Jesus Christ—of the One who said that in so far as anyone has done anything to one of the least of these, His brethren, one has done it unto Him (Mat. 25:40). And Paul knew in his bones that Jesus had meant it when He said that, because when he was on his way to Damascus to persecute Christ's followers, he had been blinded by the vision of a great light out of which Jesus' voice had asked, "Saul, Saul, why are you persecuting *me*?" (Acts 9:4, emphasis added). Jesus took Paul's treatment of Jesus' followers very personally. What Paul did to them he had done to Jesus Himself. And now Onesimus is one of these brothers—specifically, as a slave, presumably one of "the least of these."

Do you get what Paul is saying? "If you are a Christian master, it's OK for you to have a slave—as long as you treat him like Jesus." Oh, wait.

Paul does not command Philemon to set Onesimus free (though he hints that he might, so Onesimus could join Paul's evangelistic team; we don't know whether that ever happened). That choice he leaves to

Philemon. But Philemon's relationship to Onesimus can never be the same. In fact, if Philemon lets that change go forward to a place of consistency, Onesimus can no longer be a slave as that term is normally understood. The ground has been taken out from under the whole institution of chattel slavery in a way that must eventually do away with it altogether.

We don't know what became of Philemon and Onesimus. We do know that most people at the time did not get the implications of Paul's exhortation as I have brought them out here. Because of the influence of human culture and the perversity and stubbornness of the human heart, it took many centuries for the seeds Paul had planted to bear fruit. But the fruit it bore was William Wilberforce. It is no accident that the two most powerful voices leading to the abolition of the slave trade belonged to Wilberforce, the Christian member of parliament, and to John Newton, the ex-slave trader whose conversion to Christ caused him to repudiate his former profession and use his influence as a Christian minister against it. Whether he knew it or not, Paul had set the clock that led to that moment ticking when he sent Onesimus back to his master seventeen centuries before.

## CONCLUSION

It is sadly true that there were Christians who used the Bible to support slavery. But it is equally true that men with a better understanding of what the Bible actually teaches used their influence to end it. Does the Bible support slavery? Only for those who read it very superficially. It is tragic that it took so long, but it was actually the Bible that ended slavery as an official institution in Western lands. Christians have no need to be ashamed of that!

# CHAPTER 14

## "Doesn't the Bible support homophobia?"

The Bible teaches in both Testaments that homosexual acts are sin. It does not teach hatred of homosexuals (or any other sinner). But the climate today is such that even making the first claim is heard as hateful. That is why this issue takes a lot of careful unpacking. I'm going to approach it through a series of Socratic questions.

EXPLANATION:

One of the frustrations encountered by Christians trying to maintain a consistent witness today is that many of our contemporaries are so hostile to any presentation of the biblical view of human sexuality (see objection 1) that they will probably not listen to a direct proclamation of it and will consider it offensive however gently and lovingly it is given. But they will find it harder to be offended by questions. It is difficult to be offended when you are given the compliment of being asked for your opinion!

Socrates was the ancient philosopher who was famous for teaching by asking questions. He gave his name to the "Socratic method," but there was an even better practitioner of it who came later and blessed it by His example: the Lord Jesus Christ Himself. How can we follow their example in our own situation? Well–designed Socratic questions can help to defuse tense encounters and also give non-believers the opportunity to encounter a different view without rejecting it out of hand before they even hear it. Here are some possibly useful questions related to the five most common objections to the biblical position on homosexuality. Simply asking them will not convince anyone, but they can be fruitful in opening up a dialog that might, a dialog that without them might be very difficult to get started.

**OBJECTION 1:** *Any criticism of the LGBT lifestyle is homophobia and hate speech!*

**Question 1A:** Do you really believe I think less of a person just for having a different set of temptations than I do?

This question raises a crucial point. We are not singling homosexuals out as worse sinners than anyone else. We put ourselves on the same level that they occupy, just as desperately in need of God's grace as they are. They do not perceive this truth at all—because some of us don't perceive it, either. We had better be sure that we do.

**Question 1B:** If I believed you were heading off a cliff, and I said nothing to stop you, would that be, say, loving—or hateful?

Just asking this question will not convince anyone that homosexuality is disordered, or probably even that critiques of it are not hateful. It is a first step toward that conversation. We are trying to get people to reevaluate the assumption that any critique of the homosexual lifestyle is *automatically* hateful and could not possibly be anything else. We are trying to get that conversation started.

**Question 1C:** Have you heard of the fallacy of *Poisoning the Well*? Is it possible you are unintentionally committing it?

Poisoning the Well is preemptively setting a statement up for failure before anyone even has the chance to make it. "Have you stopped beating your wife yet?" If you answer yes, you admit you have been beating her. If you answer no, you admit you still are. No answer that doesn't sound bad is possible. "Only an idiot would oppose this bill!" You are listed as an idiot for opposing it before you ever even open your mouth. My favorite example is from Chaucer's "The Pardoner's Tale." The Pardoner is a medieval con man selling relics and indulgences. He claims miraculous powers for his relics but then warns, "If anyone has committed some sin so horrible that he has never confessed it, these relics will have no power in that case." If you come back the next day complaining that the relic didn't work, what will everyone assume?

We have to be careful with this question. It is too easy to bring up logical fallacies in a "gotcha!" spirit. That will backfire in a heartbeat. Nevertheless, Objection 1 does commit this fallacy by its very nature, and at some point that realization needs to be made.

**OBJECTION 2:** *Why don't you abstain from shellfish and from wearing mixed fabrics? You have no credibility unless you obey* all *of Scripture!*

**Question 2A:** Have you ever heard of progressive revelation? Do you think God could have revealed everything we needed to know about Him all at once?

In all probability, your conversation partner has not heard of progressive revelation. The second part of this question will help him or her see the relevance of the concept. Most people have never thought of revelation as a historical process. They think of the Bible the way some of us unfortunately treat it—as a kind of encyclopedia of religious pronouncements rather than as a *story* with beginning, middle, and end, a plot with an arc taking us somewhere (from creation to the fall to

redemption and restoration). It is important then that his question lead to the next one.

**Question 2B:** If not, is it possible that some practices might have been appropriate for an earlier stage of that revelation but be made obsolete by later stages?

It will be hard to deny that this is at least a reasonable theoretical possibility. It is one the person using this objection has obviously never thought of. And it leads to the next question, which is the bottom line.

**Question 2C:** Do you think it is possible that the Bible might actually tell us which practices this is true of and which it is not? Where might it do that?

If we are going to go down this road, we had better know where it does that ourselves. Relevant passages include the following: **Acts 10:9-15** (Peter receives his vision of the sheets in which God declares all foods clean[27]); **Gal. 2:14-18** (Paul rebukes Peter for trying to impose Jewish customs on Gentiles); **Col. 2:16-17** (Paul says to "Let no one act as your judge" with respect to the feast days of the Ceremonial Law); **1 Tim. 4:1-4** (Everything created by God is good and to be received with thanksgiving); **Heb. 10:1-18** (The Old-Testament sacrificial system is rendered moot because it has been fulfilled in Christ).

**Summary:** The Old-Testament Law had two parts, as we see in hindsight: the Ceremonial Law (intended for the situation in the context of salvation history in which the Old-Testament saints found themselves) and the Moral Law (universal and eternal moral principles based on God's character). The Ceremonial Law has fulfilled its purpose with the crucifixion of Christ and need no longer be followed; the Moral Law (including sexual morality) is always valid and hence still in effect. We realize that this distinction obtains because of the way different Old-Testament laws are treated in the New Testament, and because of the rationale it gives for this difference in treatment. Bottom line: The New Testament overturns the dietary and other ceremonial provisions. That is why Christians are free to eat shrimp, cheeseburgers, and pork. They are not in fact being inconsistent

---

27 Note that the primary purpose of this passage is to teach the Jews that Gentiles must now be accepted as full members of the Body of Christ without having first to convert to Judaism. A change in the status of the Jewish ceremonial law, including the laws about what foods are considered "clean," is implied in and entailed by that change, as indicated by the analogy used. Otherwise, Gentile believers could never be fully accepted and integrated into the Body.

or arbitrary at all when they do so, but rather understanding the Old Testament in the light of the *whole* of Scripture, unlike their critics. But The New Testament not only does not overturn Old-Testament teaching on homosexual practice; it actually confirms it (see objection 3).

**OBJECTION 3:** *The New Testament does not condemn faithful homosexual relationships, only promiscuous ones or male cult prostitution.*

**Question 3A:** Where exactly is this distinction made in the New Testament? Is it in Rom. 1:26-7? Is it in 1 Cor. 6:9-11? Could you show it to me there, please—in the actual wording of the text, not in assumptions imported into it?

**Commentary:** **Rom. 1:26-7** is part of a list of sins that continues in verses **29-31**. They are not *ceremonies* attendant on the idolatry of vs. **23**, but rather disordered *lusts* (vs. **24**) that result from idolatrously rejecting the truth about God. *Cult* prostitution is therefore a red herring (i.e., an irrelevant side-track). **1 Cor. 6:9** is part of a similar list, examples of the unrighteousness that is inconsistent with the Kingdom. In both cases homosexual activity is seen as sinful *per se*, not just in certain special cases. It is not, moreover, treated differently from the other sins in the lists.

**Question 3B:** Is it possible then that you might be reading that distinction *into* these passages rather than out of them?

It is very possible! As with the fallacy of poisoning the well, it is also once again important not to pounce triumphantly on your friends here. (Note the way this question is phrased: "Is it *possible* that you *might* be . . .") If your friends do not come to this conclusion on their own, it will not help them become open to reconsidering the biblical view.

**OBJECTION 4:** *Jesus says nothing about homosexuality.*

**Question 4A:** Did Jesus say anything about *marriage*?

**Hint:** Yes, He did. And all those statements presuppose traditional marriage between a man and a woman as ordained by God in Genesis.

**Question 4B:** Was Jesus at all shy or timid about opposing Jewish interpretations of the Old Testament with which He did not agree? If not, then if He does not address something, what does that silence actually imply?

**Commentary:** Jesus was in fact so bold and forthright in his opposition to contemporary religious concepts he disagreed with that He got Himself lynched as a dangerous heretic. If He had disagreed with his contemporaries' interpretation of the prohibition of homosexual practice in the Old Testament, He very probably would have said so. An argument

from silence (*argumentum ex silentio*) can never be conclusive. Jesus' silence on homosexuality therefore cannot be used to signal approval of it; if it means anything at all, the fact that He did not speak to the issue must logically be held to *support* the Old-Testament teaching, not to overturn it.

**Question 4C:** Did Jesus authorize the Apostles to speak for Him? Do *they* have anything to say on the subject?

**Note:** Yes, He did. And yes, they did. See the questions and commentaries related to Objection 3.

**OBJECTION 5:** *It is unfair to condemn people for an orientation they did not choose and cannot help.*

**Question 5A:** I did not choose to be greedy and I cannot help wanting things. Does that make it OK for me to take them? I.e., should kleptomaniacs be allowed to steal because they believe they can't help it?

**Question 5B:** If I did not choose to be heterosexual or to desire more women than I am actually allowed to have, does that make it OK for me to have them?

**Note:** The question of whether or not homosexual orientation is genetic and unchosen is worth pursuing, but not here. You will only end up tossing contradictory studies and data at each other and it will be nearly impossible to reach a conclusion. The more important point to make—and an easier one—is that even if the orientation is *not* a choice, the conclusion gay advocates wish to draw from that alleged fact does not follow from it. Whether an act is right or wrong, whether the impulse to that act should be acted on or resisted, simply has nothing whatever to do with whether or not we chose to have that impulse. We see that in almost every other context. Homosexual desires are no different. They simply cannot be justified by this argument.

**CONCLUSION:**

No, the Bible does not support homophobia. It does not treat homosexual acts any differently from any other sin. It does not allow us to think worse of a person whose temptations are different from our own, nor to mistreat such a person. But it does teach that homosexual desires are disordered and that homosexual acts are sinful, and it offers to those guilty of them the same forgiveness and redemption that it offers to those guilty of any other sin.

Nevertheless, the climate in which we live makes it especially difficult to see or even to express meaningfully the Bible's message. Increasingly

these questions and their answers will be needed in dealing not only with secular people but also with confused Christians. To be effective with either group, they must be asked out of a genuine desire for dialog, not in a "gotcha" spirit. So think beforehand about how you might want to guide the discussion that ensues, fortify yourself with prayer and study, and then try them out![28]

Again, Christian publishing House has the go to book on this subject that offers you a deeper biblical viewpoint.

HOMOSEXUALITY - The BIBLE and the CHRISTIAN: Basic Bible Doctrines of the Christian Faith by Edward D. Andrews

(ISBN-13: 978- 0692702345)

---

[28] For further discussion of this difficult topic, see Paul Copan, *When God Goes to Starbucks: A Guide to Everyday Apologetics* (Grand Rapids: Baker, 2008), pp. 77-118.

# CHAPTER 15

## "Doesn't the Bible support the oppression and abuse of women?"

As we have seen in previous chapters, it is easy to take biblical statements out of context and make it look like the Bible supports evils like genocide, racism, slavery, or homophobia. But when we read the book as a whole and in the context of its times, we discover that in fact all such charges are false. The charge of male chauvinism is no different. It exists in part because men have abused some of the Bible's teachings and used them to justify real oppression of women, just as they falsely used other passages to support slavery. But it is just as false.

What the Bible does teach about gender roles is not what modern secular feminists and Evangelical egalitarians want to hear. It is not what male chauvinists want to hear either. Both groups sometimes in support of their own ideologies twist the Bible's teaching into something just as foreign to its real meaning as that given by their opponents. When we have understood that teaching, we will discover that, if we can accept it, it is the key to human thriving just as every other biblical teaching is. I will try to lay it out in five theses, starting with a passage that has often been a bone of contention.

Some vocabulary before we begin. *Hierarchy* means a structure in which some people have authority over others; *hierarchicalism* is the view that the Bible teaches such an authority structure in the church and the home. *Complementarianism* agrees that there is such a structure, but it emphasizes strongly that the differences are only differences of role, not of worth or value. *Egalitarianism* is the view that there is no such authority structure. Everyone is equal in value and there are no distinctions in function or role. We will argue that complementarianism is the biblical position, and that it is not a form of oppression when rightly understood.

Eph. 5:21 *And be subject to one another in the fear of Christ.* 22 *Wives,* be subject *to your own husbands as to the Lord.* 23 *For the husband is the head of the wife, as Christ also is of the church, He Himself being the Savior of the body.* 24 *But just as the church is subject to Christ, so also the wives ought to be to their husbands in everything* (NASB).

Perhaps no passage of Scripture has been more misunderstood, more disastrously applied, and hence more feared by both congregation and preacher than Eph. 5:22-24. The traditional (hierarchical) understanding is so tainted by misapplication and abuse that it can hardly be heard without distortion; and the new (egalitarian) understanding is so skewed by reaction against the traditional—or against how the traditional account is perceived—that it is equally unable to help us hear the Word of God clearly. Therefore, a new beginning is needed, a fresh start. This we will attempt in this chapter—or at least the beginning of this new beginning. We will attempt to provide a framework that will allow the wise and sane Voice of Scripture to be heard constructively in the Church once again. And we will do this by propounding five theses about this passage.[29]

### THESIS I. THE BIBLE IS AN UNAVOIDABLY HIERARCHICAL BOOK, BUT NOT AS MAN UNDERSTANDS (OR THINKS HE UNDERSTANDS) HIERARCHY.

The biblical concept of hierarchy is modeled by the very Trinity itself. In passages such as John 4:34, 5:19-23, 30, 10:30, we see the Father and the Son equal in nature, power, glory, dignity, and honor, but differentiated in role. The Son's meat and drink is to do the will of the Father. The Son obeys the Father; the Father does not obey the Son, though He may grant His requests. The Father and the Son send the Spirit; the Spirit does not send the Son or the Father. Yet the Son and the Father are one. Both their unity and their differentiation are clear. Nevertheless, the "Higher" (Commander, Sender) does not dominate the "Lower" (Obedient, Sent), but rather seeks the honor of its subordinates. The Father wants all people to honor the Son even as they honor the Father (Jn. 5:22-23).

So radically different is this Trinitarian model of hierarchy from anything that we have ever experienced in a fallen world that even our Lord could not express it without seeming to create a paradox: "The Father is greater than I; . . . I and the Father are one." This set of relationships is called by theologians the "economic subordination" of the Trinity—a subordination not of value or nature or dignity or honor, but of function or role only, voluntarily adopted through love. Though all three Persons are absolutely equal in nature, honor, and even rank (being all one God),

---

[29] For further reading on Evangelicalism's compromises with the Spirit of the Age when it comes to gender, see Vernard Eller, *The Language of Canaan and the Grammar of Feminism* (Grand Rapids: Eerdmans, 1982) and John Piper and Wayne Grudem, eds., *Recovering Biblical Manhood and Womanhood: A Response to Evangelical Feminism* (Wheaton: Crossway, 1991).

nevertheless, they are not interchangeable or redundant: The Father initiates, the Son accomplishes, and the Spirit applies. The Son does the will of the Father, the Spirit glorifies the Son, and the Father seeks the honor of the Son. If Adam and Eve as human beings were made in the image of this God, then all our thinking about right order (i.e., hierarchy) needs to start from the way the Bible articulates the inner workings of the triune God.

Equal in nature but different in function or role: The same kind of paradox, based on the nature of God, is reflected in the Church, where there is a universal priesthood of believers, and yet where within this spiritual equality elders are set aside for rule and given double honor if they rule well (1 Tim. 5:17). Likewise, there is in this Church neither male nor female (Gal. 3:28), yet the male is head of the female as Christ is of the male and God of Christ (1 Cor. 11:3). Traditionalists would often like to ignore one of these sets of verses, and feminists the other. But neither of those options is open to us if we want to be faithful to Scripture. There males exclusively serve as elders without being in any way superior to females. And this same paradoxical hierarchy is reflected in the home (Eph. 5:23), where the husband is head of the family, and thus of the wife, whose equality with him in every way is not in the least compromised by that arrangement.

But this biblical picture is unfortunately very different from the human perversions of hierarchy created by man to feed his pride. In these human and worldly hierarchies, a difference in authority or even role implies a difference in value, it is assumed to be based on a difference in ability, and it leads to a difference in prestige. As a result, we lord it over one another like the Gentiles of Mat. 20:25-28. It was forbidden to be so among the disciples.

It was not to be so among the disciples because none of these things is at all true of the biblical model in its Trinitarian original. Nor should they be true, therefore, of its temporal reflections in the church and the home. Christian husband and Christian wife are supposed to be a living portrait of the relationship between Christ and the church. But how can they fulfill that role if they obliterate either side of the biblical order outlined above? How can they do so if hierarchy is either avoided as indistinguishable from oppression or practiced in an oppressive and unChristlike way? Nothing more distorts our presentation of the Gospel, nothing more hinders its credibility, and nothing more undermines our practice of the Christian life than our failure to get back to the place where both sides of this equation can be upheld with full value and complete harmony.

**THESIS II. HEADSHIP IS UNAVOIDABLY A LEADERSHIP POSITION, BUT NOT AS MAN UNDERSTANDS LEADERSHIP.**

Some feminists' interpreters have tried to read the word translated *head* in Ephesians 5:23 ("The husband is head of the wife as Christ is also the head of the church") as "source" and deny that it even implies a leadership role. The Greek word *kephale* can indeed mean source, as the spring is the "head" of a stream and we think of a river as having "headwaters." But the context is against that meaning here, as there is no point in exhorting someone to be "subject" to a source (vs. 22, referring back to the mutual submission of all believers to each other and applying it to the wife in the marriage relationship). No one would get the idea that being head did not involve leadership from this passage without a prior commitment to avoiding it no matter what. So the husband does have a leadership role. But what kind of leadership is he supposed to exercise?

Our model for leadership is Jesus, and His kind of leadership is defined in Mat. 20:25-28, where He contrasts what we might call the "Gentile Paradigm" of leadership ("lording it over" one's subordinates like the Gentiles do) with Christ's notion that the greatest should be the servant of all. This new Christian Paradigm of leadership is incarnated for us in John 13:1-16, where Jesus washes the disciples' feet and goes out of his way to make the point that this is done in fulfillment of his role as *Lord* and teacher (13:12-16). After washing their feet—the role of a menial servant—he asks the wonderful Socratic question, "Do you know what I have done?" (13:12). Those who continue to lead by the Gentile Paradigm, *and* those who think that male leadership must perforce exemplify the Gentile Paradigm and therefore must be replaced by an egalitarianism foreign to the Scriptures, both show that they do not understand what He had done—not in the least.

Remember this phrase, the "Gentile Paradigm." It is a mode of understanding leadership and headship that has infiltrated the traditional view of male headship in marriage and thus all too frequently caused it to become utterly unChristlike and unbiblical. Physical abuse happens, but emotional abuse is much more common as too many Christian wives are browbeaten by men who think their anatomy somehow gives them the right to get their way. I have counseled many women who have been made to feel guilty for not liking such treatment! One can understand why many secular feminists and their Christian sympathizers have come to *equate* male headship ("patriarchy") with abuse and why they feel compelled to twist the Scriptures into grotesque shapes in order to avoid it. Unfortunately, such twisting is still twisting, and it can only produce twisted results.

So how does Christ lead the Church? Even He does not follow the Gentile Paradigm, though He of all people would have a right to. How

does He lead? By loving the Church and giving Himself for her (Eph. 5:25-28). Why do we follow Him? Why do we hail Him as "Lord"? Because He first loved us and gave up His life for us. Even so ought husbands to be the heads of their families. What does this look like in practice?

Headship as leadership is not about the husband getting his way just because he is a man. It is about Christ getting *His* way, and the husband being responsible before God to see that this is what happens in his family. The husband and the wife in a healthy Christian marriage are not in a competition to see who gets his or her way. They both want Christ to get His way, and they both recognize that God has given the husband a special role of responsibility to take the lead in seeing that the family pursues that agenda together. Submission for the wife means encouraging and supporting her husband in *that*. She is responsible for the family following Christ's way too, but one of the most important ways she exercises her responsibility is by supporting her husband in the exercise of his.

**THESIS III. THE HUSBAND IS NOT ULTIMATELY GIVEN THE POSITION OF HEAD BECAUSE HE IS MORE QUALIFIED FOR IT.**

The assumption that the husband is given this role of leadership because he is more qualified for it really flows from the Gentile Paradigm, which, as we have seen, falsely equates role with worth and ability. In studying this topic, it is disappointing to see how many conservative scholars defend male headship by trying to argue that men inherently make better leaders. Even C. S. Lewis fell prey to this mistake in one of the least convincing sections of *Mere Christianity*, the end of chapter six of Book III, where men are portrayed as more objective toward those outside the family than women. No doubt some are. Maybe the majority are. But is that an adequate basis for male headship? Scripture never appeals to it.

Do men make better leaders? I do not care to dispute this claim, but simply to point out its irrelevance. Even if it were true as a generalization, that would still mean that lots of women would make better leaders than lots of men. We all know marriages in which the wife has tons more sense than the husband. Nor does Scripture teach this supposed male superiority as the rationale for its model. It is not mentioned in Ephesians 5, and even the passage often quoted in support of it (1 Tim. 2:12-14) merely says that Eve was deceived in the Garden--not that all women are generally or inherently more gullible than all men. The key to that passage is actually verse 13, referring to Adam's position of *responsibility* before God; Adam, having been made first, was head of the human race and therefore had the greater responsibility as its leader. Besides, if the Trinity is our model, there is no way to argue that the Son is any less "qualified" than the Father is to be the Initiator of the plan of Salvation.

So why assume that the wife is necessarily less qualified for leadership than the husband is? Doing so misses the point in ways that are profound. God has made the husband head of the family, and it is a mantle of responsibility he needs to take up. Trying to believe he is somehow more worthy of this responsibility than his wife is would be a distraction at best and a path to damaging folly if he were not careful. He needs to fulfill this responsibility because it has been given to him. That is really all he needs to know.

**THESIS IV. THE HUSBAND'S LEADERSHIP MUST BE SEEN IN THE CONTEXT OF EPHESIANS 5:21.**

It has often been said that the Bible was inspired by the Holy Spirit, but the chapter and verse divisions were inspired by the Devil. That is not true of course. The chapter and verse divisions were inserted by well-meaning men as an aid to finding passages, and they have served well in that role for hundreds of years. But those men were fallible, and they did not always put those breaks in the most logical places. We should remember that they were not part of the original text and are not inspired. If we don't, we may miss some very important features of context.

The passage from Ephesians five is a perfect example. Our translations almost all take their cue from the verse divisions and begin a new sentence in verse 22, "Wives, be subject to your husbands," as if we were starting a new topic. But actually there is no verb in Eph. 5:22, nor is there any period at the end of v. 21 in the original. It should literally read like this: "Being subject to one another . . . [including] wives to their own husbands." The main verb is actually way back in verse 18: "*Be filled* with the Spirit." The marks of the Spirit-filled life are then laid out through a series of participles. What are the effects of being filled with the Spirit? *Speaking* to one another in psalms, hymns, and spiritual songs; *singing* and making melody with our hearts to the Lord; always *giving thanks* for all things; and *being subject* to *one another* in the fear of Christ (Eph. 5:18-21, emphasis added).

Verse 22 is then a continuation of verse 21, and there is a close connection between them. Wifely submission is not a new topic. There should be no period, only a comma! Wifely submission is a continuation of the discussion of the *mutual* submission to Christ which results from a Spirit-filled life; it is an aspect of that mutual submission, a special application of it. In other words, before there is any submission of wife to husband, both wife and husband must already be submitting to one another in the Lord. It is all about submission to Christ, enabled by the Spirit. This includes the husband submitting to his responsibility to be the spiritual leader of the family and the wife submitting to that godly leadership. They

should have practiced for these roles by submitting to each other in the Lord as Christian brother and sister before there was any talk of a wedding. Mutual submission in the fear of Christ means that they have a mutual commitment to follow Christ, which means following whichever one of them first discerns Christ's will in the situation. If you are not already practicing that kind of spiritual friendship in the Lord, you have no business even thinking about getting married.

Wifely submission as an aspect of mutual submission means that the husband and the wife are designed to lead the family as a *team*—but it is a team with a designated *captain*. (Once again we see the two-edged nature of the truth, with both sides of it needing to be kept in balance: It is a team; the team has a captain.) The wife should be consulted as an equal partner, and she may even initiate. Part of the husband's responsibility as the leader is to listen to her and follow her advice when she is right. The bottom line is that if the family is not being led in a godly direction, it will be the husband who is first and most severely called on the carpet by God—just as it happened in Gen. 3:9.

The husband and wife are to lead the family together, then, but God holds the husband primarily responsible for making sure that their leadership takes the family in directions pleasing to God. And, like Christ, he is to do this not by barking orders but by setting an example of loving service, of godly living, of costly sacrifice. Otherwise, he is leading by the Gentile Paradigm, and that is *not* what God is commanding the wife to submit to. (How to handle less than ideal situations is a difficult topic that goes beyond the scope of this thesis, which is simply to restore an accurate picture of what the ideal is. I will touch on it, though, very briefly and tentatively, below.)

### THESIS V. WE DO THIS TO PICTURE THE RELATIONSHIP BETWEEN CHRIST AND THE CHURCH.

I promised you a new paradigm: Here it is. God wants the family to be a Drama Company in which the husband is assigned to enact the role of Christ, and the wife that of the church, so that the church and the world might understand who Christ is. Why is this role assigned to the husband? Not because he is more qualified for it or worthy of it. Who could be? No doubt it is partly because Christ was male, as Adam was. And, looking at today's church, I cannot help but wonder if it is not partly because the modern male is the least inclined to take this role. I am afraid that the Gentile Paradigm comes naturally to us males. We would not learn to lead like Christ unless we had to. And the ironic tragedy is that Satan has succeeded in so permeating the traditional hierarchical view with the Gentile Paradigm that men do in fact take on the role of Head with results

precisely opposite to those that God intended. But Scripture is plainly opposed to this as much as it is to egalitarianism and its erasing of all role distinctions.

What then does submission mean for the wife in the Christian Paradigm? It does not mean the husband has the right to give orders—any orders—and she must simply carry them out. It means she is willing to let the man lead the family in a godly direction. She will in fact encourage him to take on this God-assigned role. Even if she is more qualified for leadership herself, she will not usurp this role but graciously help her husband learn to grow into it, if he is willing.

What if the husband is not willing? What if he is abusive? If he is not willing to be a godly leader, the wife may be forced to take that role herself by default, but that is never her purpose or intention or preference. She will support and encourage her husband whenever he moves in the direction of genuine godly leadership. She will be willing to be the "straight man"—er, person—that he plays off of in developing the part. If on the other hand the situation is even worse, if the husband is abusive and unrepentant, the wife has some difficult decisions to make about protecting herself and her children. Nothing I can say here will make them easier. But she should not compound her situation and make it even more difficult by feeling guilty that somehow the husband's sin is her fault or by feeling that God wants her to "submit" to a situation that was never commanded. Surely the church needs to do a better job of preparing people for marriage by teaching Ephesians 5 correctly so that these abusive situations never get a chance to get started.

Our focus here is not solving all the problems of abuse but rather of restoring an accurate picture of the ideal as Scripture actually teaches it. So let us focus on these drama companies presenting the biblical pageant of Christ and the church. If both partners are playing the part they have been assigned, the husband will not be imposing his agenda on the wife, but they will be finding Christ's agenda together. For her, it means allowing someone who is her equal, not her superior, to lead in the dance. But it must be the dance tune Scripture is playing, not just any whim the husband happens to have. Now, that would be a powerful picture of Christ and the church indeed!

## CONCLUSION

Did I model what I am teaching here in my own marriage? Not always. Not as well as I wish I had, especially early on when I was myself more tainted by the Gentile Paradigm than was at all good for the relationship. Where, I can imagine someone asking in despair, do we see such a thing as

you are talking about? I would like to say, here. In your house, your congregation, and mine. Already the foretaste, increasingly the fullness. From now on. By the grace of God, let there be a new beginning in this vexed matter, in your family and mine. For this mystery is great: I am speaking of Christ and the Church.

# CHAPTER 16

## "There are so many religions, all sincerely seeking the same goal. What makes you Christians so arrogant that you think yours is the only way?"

First, is it true that all religions are seeking same goal? Maybe instead of just assuming the answer to such an important question, we should go and ask them.

Most Westerners assume that all religions are seeking the same goal, or are just "different roads to the same place," because they have only a very vague idea of what religion is all about that they absorbed without much thought from the lowest common denominator of the nominal Judaism and Christianity that surrounds them. They then proceed to read that idea into other religions where it may not fit at all.

### THE SAME GOAL?

Do all religions have the same goal? Well, isn't religion about the next life? Christians want to go to Heaven, and Hindus and Buddhists want to go to Nirvana, right? But when you actually study Eastern religion you find out that Nirvana is not about the next *life* at all. Nirvana is a form of "enlightenment" in which you realize that your existence as an individual person was an illusion. Your spirit is really part of the impersonal cosmic Everything, but because you falsely think your individual existence is real, you have individual desires. You want to have stuff that somebody else does not have. These desires ultimately cannot be fulfilled, and therefore you experience deprivation and suffering. In Nirvana, however, your soul is absorbed back into The One, Brahman, like a raindrop being absorbed into the ocean. You are then at peace because you have no more desire—but this peace (*shanti*) comes at a pretty high price. Your individuality no longer exists. Your personal ego, your individual consciousness, your awareness of you being you, is not there to enjoy that peace. *You* are not there to enjoy that peace!

I'm not making this up. The Hindu scriptures say,

> And as these juices [from the different flowers that have been made into honey] have no discrimination so that they might

> say, "I am the juice of this tree or that," in the same manner, my son, all these creatures, when they have become merged in the True (either in deep sleep or in death) know not that they are merged in the True. . . . And as those rivers, when they are in the sea, do not know, "I am this or that river," In the same manner, my son, all these creatures, when they have come back from the True, know not that they have come back from the True.[30]

The goal for Eastern religion, then, is not eternal "life" at all; it is the very opposite, non-existence (as an individual, self-conscious person). "Beyond the Person there is nothing—this is the goal, the highest road."[31] Christianity is about the fulfillment of individual personhood, which was created in the image of a personal God. But Buddhism in its original form had no place for gods, and the gods of Hinduism are manifestations whose "personality" is as much an illusion as that of their worshippers.

If personality isn't ultimately real, what does that say about love? Krishna tells Arjuna, "I am indifferent to all born beings; there is none whom I hate, none whom I love."[32] For Christianity, the goal is love experienced in personal relationship with God for all eternity. "This is life eternal, that they might know thee, the only true God, and Jesus Christ whom thou hast sent" (John 17:3). Christians are to live in love with their fellow man in this life on the way to that Heaven because "God is love" (1 John 4:8). This makes sense for Christians because their God, the ultimate *Person*, is the foundation and source of all reality. Hindus and Buddhists learn to practice not love but indifference in this life because their concept of ultimate reality is *impersonal*. Because of that, complete detachment from desire is the essence of the escape from the burden of reincarnation they aspire to. (You keep getting reborn until you figure out how to escape from the cycle of life by realizing that you don't actually exist, and since each reincarnation involves unfulfilled desire, they get to be rather a drag.)

The same goal? The only thing these two visions have in common is that the nature of the divine as they conceive it determines the goal pursued in this life and the next. Is it the same goal? Is the fulfillment of personality the same as the negation and annihilation of personality? Nothing could be further from the truth.

---

30 Nicol MacNicol, ed. *Hindu Scriptures: Hymns from the Rigveda, Five Uphanishads, The Bagavadgita* (London: Everyman's Library, 1948), p. 171.

31 Ibid., p. 201.

32 Ibid., p. 257.

Broadening our search to the goals pursued by other religions only confirms the profound misunderstanding of all of them that the person who thinks they are pursuing the same goal must have. Eternal life? Ancient pagans believed in the immortality of the soul, but their fertility religions were not about improving the quality of the existence it would have in Hades. The goal of their rituals was a better harvest at the end of the growing season here and now.

Christianity and Judaism start with a personal God who made human beings in His own image for fellowship with Him. That fellowship depicted in the Garden was broken by sin, and the whole religion is about how it can be restored. (Christians would say that Judaism is incomplete Christianity and Christianity completed Judaism.) Especially for Christianity, the goal is *love*, as Jesus, the ultimate revelation of God to men, calls the Disciples his friends (John 15:15). Islam steals the concept of a personal God from biblical religion, but its emphasis is not on love in a personal relationship but *submission* to the inscrutable will of Allah. The very word *Islam* means "submission." Although they both use the word God (*Allah* is just the Arabic word for God, cognate with the Hebrew *Elohim*), they do not think of God in the same way at all.

In sum, we can only conclude that the person who thinks that all religions have the same goal, or that they even conceptualize their goals in ways adherents of other religions would recognize, is simply a person who is ignorant of religion.

## THE ONLY WAY?

If we once get it into our heads that all religions are not just different paths to the same place—many of them are trying to go to very different places—then the whole question of whether one of them could be the only way appears in a very different light. The path you need to take depends on where you want to go, getting there depends on finding the right one, and finding the right one depends on asking the right questions. The question then becomes, not whether I want to go to Atlanta from Toccoa by car, bus, train, or plane, but whether I want to go to Atlanta, GA, or Greenville, SC. My town of Toccoa is located halfway between those two cities. (Which one represents Heaven in this analogy? Atlanta, because it is my hometown and because there is really only one road from Toccoa that will take you there, while there are a couple that you can use to go to Greenville. I like Greenville, and it is not like Hell in any other way. Sorry, South Carolina. It 's just an illustration.)

I can take a lot of roads out of Toccoa, or at least pick them up nearby: I-85 (South or North), U.S. 441 (South or North), GA. 78 South (or North), Ga. 17 (South or North), U.S. 123 (East or West). Only one of them will take me to Atlanta. If you want to get there, you had better take the right one. And if I tell you that if you want to get to Atlanta you need to take U.S. 365 to I-985 to I-85 South, and not take any of those other roads, I am just telling you the truth. And if I refuse to send you by any of those other routes, I am not being arrogant. I am just being a good neighbor. The Great Smoky Mountains National Park (U.S. 441 North) is a wonderful place and a great destination (Hey, it might be a better illustration of heaven! Oh, never mind.), but it is not Atlanta.

Christians do not claim that Christianity is the only way because they think they are smarter than everyone else and are therefore the only people who got the right answer to the question everybody is asking. They understand that everybody is not even asking the same question. They claim Christianity is the only way to truth, to meaning and purpose in this life, and to eternity with God in the next, because that is the question they want to answer. They want you to be asking that question because they think it has the best answer you could possibly find. They think Christianity is the one and only right answer to it because they trust Jesus. They trust Jesus for all the reasons we have been giving throughout this book.

If Christians are right about Jesus, He is the only founder of a world religion who was actually in a position to see the cosmic roadmap. That is, He was not just an intelligent human being trying to figure God out and doing it more convincingly than someone else; He was the Son of God. So if you don't get your directions from Him, you will be a victim of the blind leading the blind. And how did He answer this question? He said, "I am the way, the truth, and the life. No man comes to the Father but through me" (John 14:6).

## CONCLUSION:

When you actually study the religions of the world, you realize that they are not trying to go to the same place at all. They have very different ideas of the place to which they are trying to help you go. It is actually insulting to them to say that in effect they are all just different versions of the same thing. We should respect them by taking their teachings seriously. And when we do, we will realize that only one of them (at most) can be true. We want to find *that* one and follow it.

Christianity has at least two solid claims to be that faith, two claims that are relevant to the discussion in this chapter. First, it promises to take us to a place that actually fulfills our nature as human beings—that is, as

*persons*, created for relationship and love. It offers the *fulfillment* of personality in an eternal relationship of love—not the *annihilation* of it—as the final solution to our problems. I for one will not accept anything less than the Christian hope of personal fulfillment unless I am forced to believe that the Christian promise is false. Is it false? Could it be true? How could we know? Well, the Christian promise at least starts by fitting who I know myself to be: a *person* who finds my deepest fulfillment in relationship with other persons. If there is an ultimate fulfillment of that nature, it would have to be in a relationship with the ultimate Person. Christianity makes by far the best promise. Can it deliver?

In a word, yes. The second claim is that Christianity is the only religion backed up by evidence. The Christian God is not just a mythological figure. He sticks His neck out, as it were, in history. Nobody knows when Krishna walked the earth, if he ever did. Jesus on the other hand was crucified by Pontius Pilate—a Roman provincial governor who would be in our history books (in a more minor role, to be sure, but there) even if that miscarriage of justice was not on his resume. As Dorothy L. Sayers put it, Jesus is the only God with a date in history.[33] We have looked at the evidence for that date in great detail in chapters such as 1, 4, 6, and 7.

The best promise—the best case for being able to back it up: Christianity is in fact literally the only Way, the only Way that can make those two claims. Christians who make the claims are not being arrogant. They are just being accurate about who Jesus is, as the evidence shows and as they have experienced Him to be in reality: The Way, the Truth, and the Life. And they are being good neighbors who do not want to give you bad directions.

Maybe we should listen to them.

---

[33] Dorothy L. Sayers, *The Man Born to be King: A Play-Cycle on the Life of our Lord and Saviour Jesus Christ* (Grand Rapids: Eerdmans, 1944), p. 5.

# CHAPTER 17

# "What about those who have never heard the Gospel?"

Well, first, what is the Gospel? It is the Good News that there is salvation in Christ. Salvation? From what? Why do we even need to be saved?

## THE GOSPEL

The Bible says that all human beings are sinners. We have all broken God's moral law, summarized in the Ten Commandments. Indeed, if we really understand the way of life the Ten Commandments present, especially as Jesus explained it, we break those commandments on a daily basis. You have probably never committed murder, but according to Jesus hating your neighbor counts spiritually as breaking that commandment. You may not have committed adultery or fornication, but according to Jesus lust is equivalent to doing it in your heart, and that is enough to make you guilty. You probably don't steal something every day, but if Jesus is right about hate and lust, then coveting something makes you morally guilty of theft. And, of course, the very first commandment is to have no gods before God. So, is He the most important thing in your life right at this moment? Seriously? I didn't think so. If God cares as much about the state of your heart as He does about your outward acts—and according to Jesus He does—then we are all in big trouble.

So, then we are sinners, and there are consequences to sin from which we need to be saved. The Bible also says that the wages of sin is death. Because God is just, He must punish sin as it deserves, and what it deserves is the eternal death that is Hell (see chapter 19). But the Good News, the Gospel, is that God is also a God of love. So in order to show His love without compromising His justice, He sent His Son, Jesus, into the world to become a man so He could die in our place on the cross. Then to show that He accepted Christ's sacrifice, God raised Him from the dead on the third day. God could not just pretend our sin had never happened. The wages of sin had to be paid—but Christ paid it for believers. This makes it possible for God to offer forgiveness of sin to those who put their faith in Jesus, and to do it with no hint of injustice. As the Apostle Paul summarizes it, "If you confess with your mouth Jesus as Lord and believe in your heart that God raised Him from the dead, you shall be saved" (Rom. 10:9).

Those who do this are saved—that is, they are forgiven their sins, exempted from eternal punishment in Hell, adopted as God's sons and daughters, and granted eternal life with Him in Heaven.

So far, so good. Our sinfulness is pretty bad news, but even if the punishment for it may seem harsh, nobody has to experience that punishment. Forgiveness is offered as a free gift to be received by faith in Jesus. And, as God has paid an astoundingly high price to be able to make that offer, we can have a greater appreciation of His love (along with a greater respect for His justice) than if He had simply ignored our sins and let us off. That would have been mere indulgence, not the profound love God has actually shown us in Christ. If you can believe that this Gospel is true (and we have been showing reasons throughout this book why we should), then it is Good News indeed.

Nevertheless, there is still a potential problem that bothers a lot of people. Salvation, as we have seen, is offered to those who confess Jesus as Lord and believe in Him. But there have been large numbers of people throughout history, and there are still large numbers today, who live in places where they do not have access to this News. How are they supposed to confess Jesus as Lord and believe in Him if they have never heard of Him? Is it fair for God to send them to Hell if they have never even had a chance to repent and believe? How loving is a Gospel that leaves half of the members of the human race lost with no chance of salvation even if they wanted it?

Christ commanded His followers to go into all the world and preach the Gospel to everyone and make disciples of all nations. But while some of them have worked really hard to obey this commandment, they still have not reached everyone—not even close. So what about those who have never heard the Gospel? If we aren't careful, the God who a minute ago looked incredibly generous to offer salvation at all can suddenly seem arbitrary, distant, and uncaring if not positively unfair. This perspective is a stumbling block to many people who are considering the Gospel and a source of nagging doubt to many who believe it.

Let's look at one attempt to get past this difficulty that runs into problems with Scripture, and then suggest another one that does not.

## INCLUSIVISM

An increasingly popular theological position today is called *inclusivism*. It is especially popular with young people who think it makes God look more compassionate. Inclusivism overlaps much more with traditional orthodoxy than *universalism*, the idea that everyone will

ultimately be saved. Still, it tries to "include" at least some people who on the traditional view would have been lost.

Inclusivism starts at the same place as the traditional view: All human beings are sinners and need salvation. God has provided salvation through the sacrifice of Christ. This salvation is given as a free gift to those who put their faith in Him. We are commanded to share this Good News with all men and women so that they might be saved. There the traditional understanding of the Bible stops. But inclusivism adds another step. OK, it argues, people can only be saved by the blood of Christ. But what if people who have never heard of Christ can be saved (by His blood) without actually knowing His name? What if they could be saved by faith in God in terms of the light they had? Surely, inclusivists think, God would not reject a person who was sincerely seeking Him just because no missionary had ever made it to that person's tribe to give him the Gospel.

The great Christian apologist C. S. Lewis seems to have held this view. In *Mere Christianity* he speculated that there might be people in other religions who were being led by God's "secret influence" to focus on those parts of their religion that agree with Christianity, and who thus "belong to Christ without knowing it."[34] Then in *The Last Battle* he gives us a character who exemplifies this possibility. Emeth has spent his whole life thinking he was a worshiper of Tash, the cruel demonic god of the Calormenes, but after his death he is surprised to find himself in Aslan's Country (Heaven) accepted by Aslan. Aslan explains that he has accepted the service Emeth thought he was rendering to Tash:

> Not because he and I are one, but because we are opposites, I take to me the service which thou hast done to him. For I and he are of such different kinds that no service which is vile can be done to me, and none which is not vile can be done to him. Therefore if any man swear by Tash and keep the oath for the oath's sake, it is by me he has truly sworn, though he know it not, and it is I who truly reward him. . . . Unless thy desire had been for me thou wouldst not have sought so long or so truly. For all find what they truly seek.[35]

---

[34] C. S. Lewis, *Mere Christianity* (N.Y.: MacMillan, 1943), p. 176. For a critique of Lewis's view, see Donald T. Williams, *Deeper Magic: The Theology behind the Writings of C. S. Lewis* (Baltimore: Square Halo Books, 2016), pp. 168-71, 252.

[35] C. S. Lewis, *The Last Battle* (N.Y.: HarperCollins, 1956), pp. 205-6.

# CRITIQUE OF INCLUSIVISM

It is easy to see why inclusivism is an attractive position to many young Evangelicals. It seems to preserve the essential points of Evangelical orthodoxy while making God seem more open and welcoming. Unfortunately, we run into some serious problems when we try to find this view in Scripture.

One attempt is to appeal to the use of general revelation in the opening chapters of Paul's Epistle to the Romans. ("General revelation" is the way God is revealed "generally" to everyone through nature and conscience, as opposed to "special revelation," i.e., Scripture, which only comes to some.) God's existence and divine nature are seen in nature through its intelligent design (Rom. 1:20) and the Law of God is written in the hearts of Gentiles who did not have the Law of Moses (2:14-15). Why couldn't some Gentiles be accepted by responding in faith to that revelation which they had access to, even though the more specific information of the Gospel had not reached their ears?

This reasoning might sound plausible until you pay attention to the context of Romans rather than merely taking those verses as soundbytes isolated from the linear argument of which they are a part. The place where Paul is going with all of this is that all people, Jews and Gentiles alike, are included in the category of sinners (3:9), and that they are without excuse (1:20). The knowledge of God that Nature *would* give us if we were paying attention, and the Law of God written in our hearts, are not being presented as an alternative path to salvation but as that which renders us all without excuse. The response of the Gentiles to general revelation was that "their foolish heart was darkened" (1:21) because they unrighteously "suppressed the truth" (1:18). When you follow the arc of the linear argument Paul is laying out, general revelation does not give the Gentiles their own path to salvation at all. Its function is to take away their excuses just as the Mosaic Law takes away the excuse of the Jews. The point is to drive us all to Romans 3:23, "for all have sinned," so that we are all conscious of our radical need for the salvation that is offered in Jesus Christ.

That salvation is then discussed in great detail, and God has Paul make a very specific promise about it for Him in one of the most definitive summaries of the Gospel in all of Scripture. "If you confess with your mouth Jesus as Lord and believe in your heart that God raised Him from the dead, you shall be saved" (Rom. 10:9. This is the promise that we are encouraged to accept and that we are authorized to make to others. Finally the question of those who have not heard the promise comes up:

> How then will they call on Him in whom they have not believed? How will they believe in Him whom they have not heard? And how will they hear without a preacher? How will they preach unless they are sent? Just as it is written, "How beautiful are the feet of those who bring good tidings!" . . . So faith comes by hearing, and hearing by the word of Christ. (Rom. 10:14-17)

We have here a series of rhetorical questions, each of which expects the answer, "They can't." No promise is made of salvation on any other basis than explicit faith in Christ through confessing Him with our mouth and believing in our heart. The implication is that we had therefore better go and tell the Gentiles about this promised salvation. The thrust of the whole discussion provides no basis for inclusivism *as a doctrine* at all.

## AN ALTERNATIVE TO INCLUSIVISM

Are we back then to the seemingly unfair situation of there being no hope for people who were not lucky enough to live within the sound of the Gospel? Not quite. Inclusivism as we have seen is not biblical. The compassionate alternative to the biblical view turns out to be . . . the biblical view (rightly understood)! How does that work?

If God can find a way to get Emeths into heaven I will be neither upset nor surprised. What we must realize is the sobering fact that we have no *promise* of salvation for anyone except on one basis: explicit faith in Christ. I am responsible to deliver the promise God authorized me to make on His behalf. I am also responsible not to speculate about the possibility of some other path. If you ask me, "What must I do to be saved," I must reply, "Confess with your mouth Jesus as Lord and believe in your heart that God raised Him from the dead." If you ask me what the pagan who has never heard must do to be saved, I have no other answer that I am authorized to give. He too must confess with his mouth Jesus as Lord and believe in his heart that God raised Him from the dead. If you are concerned about his plight, the only biblical channel provided for expressing that concern is to go and tell him.

Where is the compassion in this view? It becomes evident when we think of two considerations. First, people are not sent to Hell for not believing in Jesus. They are sent to Hell for their sins, their rebellion against God. There is great compassion in providing any path to forgiveness and pardon for such rebels at all. God shows His compassion for sinners by sending His Son and offering pardon through faith in His name. He shows compassion for sinners who have not heard the Gospel by sending us to

tell them. He shows compassion for all of us by not hinting about any alternative path to salvation or making any alternative promises of Salvation. Why not? So that the pressure is on believers to carry out the Great Commission and spread the Gospel, and so that people are not tempted put their faith in false hopes. In all of this, God shows us His great compassion.

And what of those that we do not reach in time? Are they abandoned without hope altogether? Not necessarily. God will do what is right with them. If He can find an extraordinary or unusual way to apply Christ's blood and save some of them, He will. No one who truly seeks Him will be lost. But there is no *promise* of salvation made to anyone by any other route than personal and explicit faith in the name of Jesus—because God is not only truly compassionate but also truly wise.

## CONCLUSION

We then must be content to live in His wisdom. We should not teach inclusivism as a doctrine because we must not make or imply promises that God has not authorized us to make. We have all we can do to proclaim the one we were given! We can see that His mercy reaches far and wide, and we can trust that it may reach farther than we can see. We after all cannot make pronouncements on who is ultimately saved. That is His prerogative. We can however rejoice in the *assurance* of salvation that is given to those who believe. And we can rejoice in the privilege we have been given of proclaiming that assurance through the Gospel.

Let us do so.

# CHAPTER 18

# "If God is a God of love, why did he let my loved one die?"

I have given above a very intense and specific version of a more general question. If God is so loving, why does He let bad things happen to people? Why did He create a world so badly designed that sad, even tragic, even evil events are commonplace in it? In a world ravaged by cancer, AIDS, war, famine, corruption, oppression, rape, murder, and other forms of violence, does it even make sense to talk about a God of love being behind such a world? In the West we have been relatively protected from such things. But if you have traveled in third-world countries you have seen blind people begging on the streets and men whose legs were rendered useless by polio pushing themselves along the streets with their hands while seated on skateboards. Even in the West, we do not have to go back that far in our own history to encounter similar conditions. Many of the thousands of wounds suffered in the American Civil War led to amputations, all those operations were performed without anesthesia, and all those men lived out their lives as cripples, without the benefit of prosthetics.

Yet despite the cumulative weight of all this general suffering, the problem of evil hits home even harder when it becomes personal—when the person suffering is you or, even worse, someone you love. This question differs from all others in that the emotional impact of our experience of evil combines with the seemingly plausible argument that skeptics bring against Christian faith from the fact of evil to make the problem of evil and suffering the biggest gun in the atheist's arsenal. Understanding the argument and being able to make a logical response to it is only the beginning. Nobody will be in a position to evaluate that response logically and objectively unless we also meet them at the point of their pain. So let's try to understand the argument and then try to give some help in dealing with the raw emotions with which this issue often leaves people.

## THE ARGUMENT

The argument is known as the problem of evil or of pain or of suffering, and the branch of theology and apologetics that tries to respond

to it is known as *theodicy*, from the Greek words for God and justice. How, atheists ask, can we believe in a God who is simultaneously loving and just in the light of the level of suffering that exists in the world? One fairly clear version of the argument goes like this:

A. If God were good, he would wish to eliminate evil.
B. If God were omnipotent, he would be able to eliminate evil.
C. But evil exists.
D. Therefore, either God is not good or he is not omnipotent.

The argument is stronger than most atheist arguments because each premise is plausible and difficult for Christians to deny, and because the conclusion seems to follow logically from the premises. No Christian wants to admit that God is not good, nor that he is not omnipotent, nor that evil does not exist. Indeed, we cannot make those admissions, because the Bible teaches all three propositions. To deny any one of them is to deny the Christian faith; yet together they seem to lead to a place that also denies the faith. If good does not mean opposition to evil, what does it mean? We do not believe that God is incapable of eliminating evil. In fact, we promise that He will do just that—but only after the Second Coming. Why not now? So, the argument goes, if God could eliminate evil but does not, His goodness is compromised. If He wants to eliminate evil but cannot, His omnipotence goes down the tubes. Of course, there is no contradiction if He simply doesn't exist. On every one of these scenarios, it is argued that traditional Christian teaching is simply incoherent. It leads to an inevitable contradiction, skeptics maintain, and therefore must be false.

## THE RESPONSE: ROUND ONE

Normally if you want to refute an argument, you must either show that one of its premises is factually false, or else that it commits a logical fallacy in drawing its conclusion from those premises. It is not easy to make either of those moves against this argument. If neither of those options is available, it's not quite game over, however. You could show that the argument misunderstands one of the key terms, in which case that premise might be technically true, but not in the sense required by the argument. You could also show that it has left some important factor out of consideration. Christians typically make both of those moves in response to the argument from evil.

One term that certainly needs some definition is *omnipotence*. In the atheist's argument it seems to be taken to mean that God can do anything. But informed Christians have never understood God's omnipotence that way. The word comes from two roots meaning all (*omni*) and powerful

(*potence*). It means that God has unlimited power. But in Christian theology it has never meant that God can do absolutely anything. Scripture gives us a number of things that God cannot do: He cannot lie, for example (Heb. 6:18). The Bible interestingly does not say that God *does* not lie. He *can* not. It is impossible. There are other things God cannot do. God cannot not exist, He cannot change, He cannot die, He cannot fail to keep His promises, He cannot act contrary to justice. In sum, He cannot do anything that is inconsistent with His own nature and character. He can do anything that is consistent with who He is.

How does this work in practice? Here is one example. Because God is a God of truth, He cannot create a logical contradiction. God cannot draw a square circle. But this is no contradiction of omnipotence; is not a limitation of His power. More power will not help you draw a square circle, because no matter how strong you are, if you give it four corners it will not be a circle and if you make it round it will not be square. God is not *restrained* by logic as if it were something external to Him forbidding Him from drawing this square circle. Rather, it is His own nature as a God of truth that makes the law of non-contradiction universally valid. God's character as a God of truth and covenant faithfulness is the source of the laws of logic. He is omnipotent in that He can do anything He wants to do. He does not want to draw a square circle. Unlike us, He knows better. As C. S. Lewis put it brilliantly, "Meaningless combinations of words [like "square circle"] do not suddenly acquire meaning simply because we prefix to them the two other words 'God can.'"[36]

How then does this definition help with the problem of evil? Eliminating evil is not a logical contradiction, so it is something God could in theory do. And in fact, as we have seen, it is something Christians believe He is going to do. But there are some other relevant things that God cannot do and could not have done because they would involve logical contradictions. He cannot act unjustly. And He could not give mankind the power of choice and not give it at the same time. Human choices either have to matter or they don't. You cannot have it both ways. And if God granted to us the dignity of having our choices matter, then He could not justly shield us from the consequences of those choices if we chose disobedience to His commandments, to the moral Law. And if He provided a redemption from those consequences that works itself out in history, then there has to be history within which it can be worked out. Evil is then the result of human sin, directly in the case of moral evil and indirectly in the case of natural evil. The sacrifice of Christ makes it possible for God to

[36] C. S. Lewis, *The Problem of Pain* (N.Y.: MacMillan, 1940), p. 16.

offer forgiveness of sin in response to faith and repentance, and to do so with no compromise to His justice, because Christ has paid the penalty for sin in our behalf. And so evil is permitted to continue for a while so that we guilty sinners can have the opportunity to be saved from it by God's grace through repentance and faith.

This response is known as "The Free-Will Defense." It holds that God *permits* evil for the sake of the *greater good* of having free creatures whose choice to love and obey Him (or not) would be *meaningful*. The only way to guarantee that evil would not result would have been to create a race of robots. We would all be programmed to obey Him perfectly—and who would care? That would not have been worth doing. (Do not let the term "free will" divert you into the Calvinist/Arminian debate, by the way. We are talking about human nature in its original constitution. Calvinists and Arminians only disagree about the extent to which the power of free choice was lost as a result of Adam's fall.) Bottom line: God determined that the existence of evil was worth it given the greater good that would result. This move is biblical, for a similar argument was made by the Apostle Paul: "For I consider that the sufferings of this present time are not worthy to be compared with the glory that is to be revealed to us" (Rom. 8:18).

Is this response satisfactory? It does succeed in showing the logical possibility that God could be both omnipotent and good and still permit evil. But questions still remain. Did it have to be *this* much evil? In His infinite wisdom, could God not have found a way to achieve this greater good without exacting such a high price—including the specific instance of suffering that the doubter finds unacceptable? There is going to be a mystery of evil left after all that we can say. And to say that it is no longer logically impossible to trust God in the light of the history of evil is not necessarily to say that any one of His hurting creatures will be able to trust Him in the light of the evil he or she has suffered or is suffering. So the Free Will Defense takes us a step in the direction we need to go, but the discussion is not over by a long shot.

## THE RESPONSE: ROUND TWO

The skeptic's response to the Free Will Defense is typically an argument from what is called "gratuitous evil." Alright, the skeptic argues, it is all well and good to say that evil may be justified by a greater good. But the world does not just contain evil; it contains *gratuitous* evil. Gratuitous evil is evil that cannot be justified in terms of any greater good that supposedly follows from it. To argue that evil is justified by a greater good, you would have to be able to show three things: that there is a direct causal connection between the evil and the good that results from it,

that the good actually outweighs the evil in question, and that the good could not have been produced in any other way, without the evil. It is easy to come up with examples of evil for which it is virtually impossible for most of us to meet the three criteria. A cute little deer is horribly roasted alive in a forest fire. What is the good that results from the cruel death of Bambi? Take a tour of one of the Nazi concentration camps in Europe and contemplate the six million who died brutal and senseless deaths after being deprived of all human dignity under the sign reading "*Arbeit macht frei*" ("Work sets you free"). What commensurate good came of that? You can't just point to the existence of the nation of Israel. Is it really clear that it fully compensates the victims for their pain? And besides, many will not even see Israel as a clear example of good. Many Christians are either reduced to silence by such arguments or find themselves sputtering responses that sound lame at best.

Is the argument from gratuitous evil a slam dunk, then? No. As impressive as it sounds, it has a couple of serious weaknesses. First, it is asking of its opponents an impossible task. What is the formula by which we calculate the position of the line that is crossed whereby a given example of evil (or the totality of evil) becomes gratuitous in relation to the magnitude of the good (human significance) that results? Nobody knows. Christians do not know, and that is why they can feel stumped by the argument. But what goes unnoticed is the fact that the skeptic does not know either. And in order to prove his case, he needs to know. But the fact is that not only do we not know, *neither of us is in a position to know.*

Why aren't we in a position to know? The lines of cause and effect in the web of events that constitutes the flow of time are incredibly complex. The future consequences of even small acts in the present are incalculable. The famous "butterfly effect"[37] can magnify good or evil consequences in ways that are utterly unpredictable. How do we even measure how much good and evil there are on a cosmic scale? Is the imbalance apparent to us in the present moment the final answer? Nobody knows. Only an omniscient skeptic would be in a position to make the argument from gratuitous evil, and only an omniscient apologist would be qualified to answer it. There is only one Person capable of evaluating this argument, and He made the decision to allow the history that is unfolding to take place. None of us is logically in a place to question that decision.

The skeptic is also usually assuming that there is a one-to-one correspondence between any specific example of evil and the specific good

---

[37] Because of the radical interconnectedness of all events, a butterfly flapping its wing in Tokyo can theoretically cause a thunderstorm in New York City.

that supposedly justifies it. That is the kind of answer he expects the Christian to supply, knowing that ultimately it cannot be done. But we do not even know that it needs to be done. We simply do not know that reality is structured that way. And even if it is, we are not in a position to offer that kind of analysis. The Christian who lets himself be maneuvered into trying to respond on this basis has taken on an impossible task. He will ultimately be expected to provide a specific justification for every example of evil that has ever happened. Sooner or later the skeptic will be able to find one that will stump him.

This is a no-win game that we should simply refuse to play. The logical justification for that refusal is the well-known impossibility of proving a negative. If you want to prove that there is such a thing as a black swan (a *positive* claim), what do you have to do? Find one. Just one. One is enough. That is doable. If you want to prove that there is *no* such thing (a *negative* claim), what do you have to do? Examine every single swan in the universe, and then have some way to be sure you did not miss one. That is not practically doable. Do not put your place in the position of having to prove that there is no black swan—i.e., no example of gratuitous evil! It is doubly impossible—because you are trying to prove a negative and because the skeptic has not been able to specify where the line is. Neither of us can play this game. Therefore, the argument from gratuitous evil (so far) ends in a draw.

## THE RESPONSE: ROUND THREE

We realize then that the skeptic is simply not capable of proving that gratuitous evil exists. All he can do is show that much of the evil we experience *seems* gratuitous *to us*, in that it is very difficult to demonstrate its justification by a greater good. It is important then to understand that what we have to overcome is not a logical argument (though it will often be presented disguised as one), but an *appearance*, a gut feeling that something is wrong with the universe. But, of course, the Christian agrees that something is wrong with the universe. The question then boils down to how we justify faith in God's goodness in spite of this appearance. Why, in other words, should we walk by faith and not by sight? I think at least three considerations justify choosing faith in Christ.

The first consideration is that, while the skeptic will not want to admit it, he is making just as much of a faith commitment as the believer is. He would like to think that logic and evidence support his belief that the universe is too evil to be the creation of a good God, while the believer just puts his trust in a fairy tale. But we have spent the whole of this chapter pointing out the holes in that idea. *Neither* of us is in a position, by reason

and experience alone, to judge whether or not any given evil is truly gratuitous. We live in a universe that contains both appalling evil and astounding goodness. We've been focused on the evil in this chapter, but we are surrounded by the goodness. Just take a breath of fresh air. At your next meal, ponder the fact that the universe produces food that not only nourishes you but gives you pleasure while doing so. The intellectual beauty of the mathematics behind natural laws is something few of us are in a position fully to appreciate, but those who can are able to use those laws to put a spacecraft on mars. Art, music, poetry, love, friendship, loyalty, heroism—all exist and are accessible to human beings. Good and evil: Neither the skeptic nor the Christian has the knowledge or the wisdom to sort through it all and balance it up. At the end of the day, do we want reality to exist or don't we? Either answer we give is based on faith. What (or who) will we trust? God or our own bitterness?

The second two considerations help us realize that while we are both making commitments of faith, they are not equally rational or wise. The skeptic does not in fact live consistently with his faith commitment—because, well, he lives. He thinks, whatever he says, that, all things added up, life is worth living. He proves this by the fact that he has stayed alive long enough to argue with you that it is not. If he really believed that the universe is an evil that cannot be justified, he would choose to stop experiencing that evil. That choice is within his power. The fact that he has not acted on it proves that on some level there is a part of him that is actually hoping that he will lose his argument with the believer. So here is the first difference between the skeptic's faith commitment and the believer's: The disciple of Jesus can live consistently with his, and the skeptic cannot. If we care enough about logic to be having this argument, that ought to tell us something.

Finally, we come to the bottom line reason why, even though I cannot prove it by adding my own experiences of good and evil up, I believe that God is good in spite of many appearances to the contrary. That reason is Jesus. He lived, and by His life He showed us the meaning of love. He died, and by His death in our place in atonement for our sins, He showed us the meaning of love—for "God .demonstrates His own love toward us, in that while we were yet sinners, Christ died for us" (Rom. 5:8). He proved that those demonstrations were not a fluke but were in fact the key to the meaning of the universe by rising from the dead.

There is one place in all the universe that I have found where this strange mixture of good and evil we call life makes sense. It is the place where the shadow of the Cross falls on the Empty Tomb. If you want to tell God that He should not have created the world, that He was wrong to

place on us the burden of suffering as a price for our significance, you need to do it while standing at the foot of the Cross looking up into the eyes of Jesus. There we realize that God did not ask us to pay any price for human significance that He was not willing to pay himself—and pay a thousand times over anything that we have ever had to bear. There I realize that trusting in the goodness and love of God even when things in my life are going horribly really does make sense.

Take your friend who is struggling with the evils of life to the foot of the Cross. Live there yourself. Take your stand there. It is the only place from which you can walk to the Empty Tomb and the paths of life.

## CONCLUSION

I have given the best answer I can to the intellectual problem of evil. Evil will always remain a mystery that we cannot fully explain. But at the Cross we discover that Good is a greater and more powerful mystery. That is a discovery worth making.

I also promised at the outset of this chapter to try to help with the emotional problem of evil. It is intertwined with the intellectual problem in that it is whole persons, not just brains, who suffer and who doubt. Often the arguments that constitute the intellectual problem are a smokescreen for the fact that people are hurting, and hurting too much to see straight. What I am about to say is relevant to all the questions people have about the faith, but especially essential here.

We must be prepared to understand the intellectual answers, in so far as we can give any. We must also be sensitive to the pain. Trying to deal with the intellectual issues when people are not ready for them can do more harm than good. It will not matter how brilliantly you give the answers I have provide above unless people can feel that you care about them. Don't bristle at their bitterness. Don't even try (at first) to counter their arguments. These people are not the Enemy; they are his victims. First, just be with them. Sit beside them and put your arm around their shoulders and weep with them. On any topic, but especially here, apologetic arguments are effective only when they fly on the wings of redemptive love. Let hurting people first wonder how you can possibly love them in spite of their bitterness against your God. Then they will be ready to wonder how Jesus can love them.

And then they are ready for that trip to the Cross.

# CHAPTER 19

# "How can it be just for God to impose an infinite punishment (Hell *forever*) for finite sins?"

Many atheists (and some Christians) object to the doctrine of Hell on the grounds that they think it is inherently unjust. How, they ask, can it be right for a good and just God to impose an eternal punishment for merely temporal sins? How, in other words, can it be just for Him to impose an infinite punishment for finite sins? For it is hard to see how human beings, being temporal and finite creatures, could commit any other kinds of sin than finite ones. But unending conscious punishment is . . . unending. Multiply any positive number by infinity, and you can begin to see the problem.

The atheist who pursues this line of reasoning finds support for his suspicion that the Christian concept of a good God is simply incoherent; the Christian who does so seeks to revise or soften or eliminate altogether the traditional doctrine of eternal punishment. And one must admit that the argument has a certain surface plausibility. People thus persuaded might well question whether traditional Christian belief really takes the goodness and justice of God with sufficient seriousness.

But what if it is actually the Questioners who do not really understand or take seriously the goodness of God?

The *goodness* of God!

How could that be?

## THE GOODNESS OF GOD

Well, what if a maximally and eternally good, wise, powerful, and holy Being who was the Creator and Sustainer of the world actually existed? He would, in other words, be more good than Frodo, wiser than Gandalf, stronger than Treebeard, more faithful than Sam, more far-seeing than Legolas. He would have more integrity than Aragorn and be more committed to all that is right and good than Faramir. He would in fact be the inexhaustible Well from which characters like those, to the extent that

they exist in the real world, draw their goodness, wisdom, power, and righteousness. He would possess such attributes infinitely, that is, inexhaustibly, by virtue of being their eternal and uncreated Source, the One who in the beginning first said, "Let there be light."

Would such a Being then not be *infinitely worthy* of all our worship, all our obedience, all our devotion, and all our adoration? Would such a Being then not *infinitely deserve* all our worship, obedience, devotion, and adoration? I mean infinitely *deserve* these responses from us, not just be in a position to demand and coerce them. That is, just by His being who and what He is, those responses would be not just nice or even desirable on our part but inherently appropriate to Him, indeed, inherently *owed* to Him. To fail to see or accept this obligation would be to be complicit in a pernicious lie about the real nature of things; to refuse this obligation would be morally culpable. And I mean by *infinitely* that there would be no conceivable limit to that worthiness and that desert on His part, and hence to that obligation on ours. He would be eternal and uncreated, hence unbounded by space or time; so there would be no limits to His possession of the attributes that justify such responses from us. All this seems to follow inexorably.

## THE OBJECTIVITY OF GOODNESS

Modern people may hit a major hurdle here, though. They tend to see attributes like *worthiness* and *desert* as subjective phenomena—as existing in the eye of the beholder rather than in the nature of the observed object. They have lived in a world where everybody gets a trophy just for showing up. They may think, "Well, if you feel God 'deserves' worship because of who He is, that's fine for you, but what does it mean for me? Why can't I just shrug my shoulders and move on? Why must I base my whole life on something *external* to *me*?" What can be said in response to that line of thinking?

People who think this way have usually not ever noticed how inconsistently they do so. (They have also probably not read chapter 9 of this book.) In fact, some of the things we think are subjective opinions ("Vanilla is tastier than chocolate") and some are objective facts ("Georgia is east of Mississippi"). Modern people tend to treat statements about moral value as belonging to the first category (vanilla vs. chocolate) because people often disagree about them, whereas most people will agree about where Georgia is on the map. But surely that assumption is a bit premature. At least some moral facts are moral *facts*, not just feelings. "Wanton cruelty to innocent children is just wrong." "Genocide (as in the Holocaust) is just wrong." It does not really matter how we feel about it. If we fail to disapprove of such things, it is not a matter of taste; it is precisely a moral

*failing* on our part. We have mistaken Georgia for Mississippi, not vanilla for chocolate.[38]

Alright, if we have to admit that there is such a thing as an objective moral value, one that demands a response from us (approval, say, or judgment) whether we feel inclined to make it or not, then surely one place where we should expect to find such an unyielding moral reality would be in the One who is the very Source and Wellspring of creation, both of its existence and its goodness. If that is the case, we are ready to return to the point established earlier: Would such a Being then not be *infinitely worthy* of all our worship, all our obedience, all our devotion, and all our adoration? Would such a Being then not *infinitely deserve* all our worship, obedience, devotion, and adoration?

## RESPONDING TO THE GOODNESS OF GOD

Alright, then, here's the next step: If all of that is true, then would stubbornly and persistently withholding those responses, indeed, stubbornly and persistently yielding them to something—to *anything*—else: Would that not then make us in a sense *infinitely guilty* of rebellion? And would that rebellion not be infinitely ungrateful and inexcusable? For there could be no conceivable limit to how wrong it was. By what possible moral calculus could we then judge Hell to be unjust? There is none. From this perspective, God's goodness is not in conflict with the justice of eternal punishment; it is the very consideration that makes its justice and rightness inescapable. Yes! God's *goodness.*

There are further questions that have to be considered. If such a Being existed and we were His creatures, absolutely dependent on Him for our own existence, would worship of, obedience to, devotion to, and adoration of Him not then be the ultimate fulfillment of our existence? Would refusing them, or giving them to anything else, not be the ultimate frustration of our nature? Would that frustration not be itself the very definition of Hell—even if no retributive justice as such were involved? For, having rejected the Source of all that is good, what could our existence then be? It would be an existence cut off from the Well from which flow the waters of life: goodness, knowledge, wisdom, strength, justice, and love. It would therefore be by its very nature an existence devoid of those things and full of evil, folly, impotence, futility, and every kind of wickedness.

---

[38] For further defense of the concept of objective value, see chapter 9 of this book and also C. S. Lewis, *The Abolition of Man* (N.Y.: MacMillan, 1947).

## HELL: THE REFUSAL OF GOODNESS

What could such an existence be but Hell? And if retributive justice were involved (it cannot be excluded as part of the picture if we are to be faithful to Scripture), who would be in a position to complain that it was unjust or undeserved? For by refusing worship, obedience, devotion, and adoration to God, by giving them to anything else, we would have received precisely what we had chosen: a life in which our aspiration for anything that is good and noble is fully and finally frustrated.

## THE EXISTENCE OF GOD

One might well object that hypothetical questions like these do not prove the existence of such a God. No. They do not. But they do clarify what the Christian claim about God is, and hence show that the traditional Christian claims about the afterlife are not inconsistent with it—indeed, are wonderfully coherent. And they can also lead to further questions: If this Being does not exist, how does it come about that anything exists? If naturalism and materialism are true, where did concepts like goodness and justice (and evil and injustice) come from? For in a naturalistic world there is no evil and no injustice—merely certain situations we do not happen to like. If naturalism is true, where did the concept of truth come from? If naturalism is true, how could naturalism (or anything else) *be* true? If naturalism is true, how could naturalism (or anything else) be *true*? For in such a world all ideas (and their antitheses) would equally be nothing more than chemical reactions in the brains of organisms which evolved to have them by chance. And who (or, more accurately, what) would judge between those ideas and their antitheses? Another set of chemical reactions subject to the same conditions is the only possible answer. As C. S. Lewis realized in *Miracles*, thinking like this leads us nowhere.[39]

Such questions might well lead to the realization that the existence of God is, at minimum, a not-unreasonable hypothesis in trying to account for the fullness of the reality we experience by living in this wondrous world. For it is a world that does contain goodness, justice, and truth, along with evil, injustice, and lies, whether a secular philosophy has room for them or can give meaning to them or not. If God makes sense, then Heaven and Hell make sense: If the world contains real and not just imagined goodness

---

[39] C. S. Lewis, *Miracles: A Preliminary Study* (N.Y.: MacMillan, 1947), esp. chp. 3.

and evil, then it makes sense that there should somewhere be ultimate fulfillments of both—that is, Heaven and Hell. Then the realization that God's existence actually makes sense of the world (and is the only thing that does) might put us in a position to receive the life, death, and resurrection of Christ in history as a solid basis for faith in the God who, the disciples were convinced, was revealed to them there in His Son.

Well, one might also object, I cannot imagine such a God. No. You cannot. Not fully, if anything I have said about Him here is true. In fact, we are warned that it can be dangerous to try. We can only safely conceive of God by sticking to the pictures of Him we are given in Scripture, culminating in the only perfect Image, His Son Jesus Christ. If we tried to imagine Him outside of that framework we would only create false and corrupted images of Him and worship them. They are technically known as *idols*. Because of the rebellion of our first ancestors we have become constitutional rebels and constitutional manufacturers and worshipers of idols. They do not have to be made of literal wood or stone to be horribly real and destructive—and to render us horribly guilty.

## CONCLUSION

Now, what if this good God loved us so much that He was not content to leave us in such a state of idolatry and rebellion and futility but had offered us a way back to Him? What if He had provided it by the sacrificial and atoning death of His Son, who had offered to absorb all the consequences due to our guilt and do it in our place? You could never find God; as a constitutional rebel, you don't even want to. But if He cut through all of your resistance and revealed Himself to you in such a way that He opened the eyes of your heart, so that you could get even the vaguest apprehension of what He really is as described above, would you not then *want* to give Him all your worship, obedience, devotion, and adoration? Such at least is the testimony of many who have had such an experience. And you will find yourself beginning, stumblingly and fitfully at first, to do so too if you are ever granted to see even the faintest glimpse the Image He gave us: of the glory of God in the face of Jesus Christ.

In other words, the justice of Hell is not really our intellectual problem. The very *goodness* of the God we despise, disobey, ignore, and hate ironically demands Hell. His goodness—the fact that He is the Wellspring and Source of all that is good, and thus infinitely deserves the worship, obedience, devotion, and adoration we have withheld from Him and given to another—demands some such fate for the reprobate every bit as much as His justice does. So, no, the justice of Hell is not the real problem. The real mystery, the thing that we can accept but never finally explain, is the

grace of Heaven. Some of us constitutional rebels, the ones who are enabled to accept it, will be forgiven and changed and granted to see Him face to face. I want to be one of those!

Don't you?[40]

Again, Christian Publishing House is offering another book which supports the eternal destruction annihilationist view because the reader should have both views. The author has been fair and balanced all through. Nevertheless, this one view is important enough to highly recommend a biblically grounded book on the subject.

WHAT WILL HAPPEN IF YOU DIE?: Should You Be Afraid of Death or of People Who Have Died? by Edward D. Andrews

(ISBN-13: 978-1-945757-83-9)

## CONCLUSION

We have tried to provide answers to some of the questions that skeptics and atheists throw at Christian believers, and which believers may wrestle with themselves. In the process I hope we have shown that none of those challenges are good reasons not to believe in Christ. I hope we have also uncovered a lot of the positive reasons why we should believe in Him as the eternal Son of God who is the Savior or the world and our personal Lord.

Why do Christians believe in God? It is because a number of independent lines of evidence—the contingency and intelligent design of the universe, the history of Israel, and their own religious experience, to mention just a few—point in the same direction. But of all those reasons, one stands out as supreme: *Jesus*. His birth, life, teachings, death, and resurrection—ultimately His Person, who He is. He is the infinite God, the eternal *Logos*, revealed in human flesh. He is the perfect image of the invisible God made visible. Christians are convinced that if you want to know whether God is, if you want to know *who* God is, if you want the most profound answers available to those questions, you just look at Jesus.

Jesus? Yes, Jesus. Period. Pure and simple.

---

[40] For further discussion of why a good God would sent people to Hell, see Paul Copan, "*That's Just Your Interpretation": Responding to Skeptics Who Challenge your Faith* (Grand Rapids: Baker, 2001), pp. 101-9, and Douglas Groothuis, *Christian Apologetics: A Comprehensive Case for Biblical Faith* (Downers Grove, Il.: InterVarsity Press, 2011), pp. 653-61..

How do we know God is personal? Because Jesus looked to Him as his Heavenly Father. How do we know He is compassionate? Because Jesus forgave the woman taken in adultery. How do we know He is faithful? Because Jesus was faithful even to death on a cross. How do we know He is powerful? Because He raised Jesus from the dead. How do we know He is consistent and trustworthy? Because Jesus came as the fulfillment of His ancient promises to Abraham and David. How do we know He is simultaneously just and gracious? Because Jesus died on the cross to pay for our sins. How do we know He is real? Because the Christ He sent was so real that you could have got a splinter in your finger from the Manger or the Cross, or stubbed your toe on the rock that (temporarily) sealed the Tomb. It all depends on Jesus; it all comes back to Jesus. He is the bottom line.

It all really does come down to that. If Jesus can't get you to believe in His heavenly Father, no one can—least of all me. What I can do is point you back to Jesus, and maybe clear up a few technical difficulties that might be preventing you from seeing him clearly. I hope I've made some progress in that direction in this book. But He is the bottom line. Some of the other reasons for believing in God are good reasons. But this one is Reason (the *Logos*) itself. Stray from Him, and the *apparent* "reasons" against faith offered by skeptics seem overwhelming. Stay focused on Him, and you can have the same faith that sustained Him beneath His crown of thorns.

Believe in Jesus with new confidence. Share Him with new boldness (and intelligence and sensitivity). And may God receive the glory.

Amen.

## Other Books for Our Youth

## Another Book By Author

ISBN-13: 978-1-945757-79-2

# Bibliography

Andrews, Edgar. *From Nothing to Nature: A Basic Guide to Evolution and Creation.* Grand Rapids: Evangelical Press, 1993.

----------. *Who Made God? Searching for a Theory of Everything.* Grand Rapids: Evangelical Press, 2009.

Archer, Gleason L., Jr. *Encyclopedia of Bible Difficulties.* Grand Rapids: Zondervan, 1982.

Bassham, Gregory, ed. *C. S. Lewis's Apologetics: Pro and Con.* Leiden: Brill/Rodopi, 2015.

Bauckham, Richard. *Jesus and the Eyewitnesses: The Gospels as Eyewitness Testimony.* Grand Rapids: Eerdmans, & Cambridge: Cambridge Univ. Pr., 2006.

Behe, Michael J. *Darwin's Black Box: The Biochemical Challenge to Evolution.* N.Y.: The Free Press, 1996.

Bradley, Keith R. "Slavery." *The Oxford Companion to Classical Civilization.* Ed. Simon Hornblower and Antony Spawforth. Oxford: Oxford University Press, 1998: 670-73.

Brown, Dan. *The Da Vinci Code.* N.Y.: Anchor Books, 2003.

Bruce, F. F. *The Canon of Scripture.* Downers Grove, IL: InterVarsity Press, 1988.

----------. *The New Testament Documents: Are They Reliable?* Downers Grove, IL: InterVarsity Press, 1960.

Campbell-Jack, W. C. and Gavin McGrath, eds. *New Dictionary of Christian Apologetics.* Downers Grove, IL: InterVarsity Press, 2006.

Chesterton, G. K. *The Everlasting Man.* NY: Dodd, Mead, and Company, 1925.

----------. *Orthodoxy.* N.Y.: Doubleday, 1959.

Copan, Paul. *"How Do You Know You're Not Wrong?" Responding to Objections that Leave Christians Speechless.* Grand Rapids: Baker, 2005.

----------. *"That's Just Your Interpretation": Responding to Skeptics Who Challenge Your Faith.* Grand Rapids: Baker, 2001.

----------. *When God Goes to Starbucks: A Guide to Everyday Apologetics.* Grand Rapids: Baker, 2008.

Collins, Francis S. *The Language of God: A Scientist Presents Evidence for Belief.* N.Y.: Free Press, 2006.

Craig, William Lane. *Reasonable Faith: Christian Truth and Apologetics*, 3rd ed. Wheaton: Crosssway, 2009.

Dembski, William A. *The Design Revolution: Answering the Toughest Questions about Intelligent Design.* Downers Grove, Il.: InterVarsity Press, 2004.

----------. *Intelligent Design: The Bridge Between Science and Theology.* Downers Grove, Il.: InterVarsity Press, 1999.

Duriez, Colin. *Francis Schaeffer: An Authentic Life.* Wheaton, Il.: Crossway, 2008.

Eller, Vernard. *The Language of Canaan and the Grammar of Feminism.* Grand Rapids: Eerdmans, 1982.

Eusebius of Caesarea. "The Life of the Blessed Emperor Constantine." ca. 340 AD. *The Nicene and Post-Nicene Fathers*, 2nd Series. Ed. Philip Schaaf. Peabody, Ma.: Hendrickson, 1995: 1:481-559.

Geisler, Norman. *Baker Encyclopedia of Apologetics.* Grand Rapids: Baker, 1999.

Geisler, Norman and Frank Turek. *I Don't Have Enough Faith to Be an Atheist.* Wheaton: Crossway, 2004.

Greenlee, J. Harold. *An Introduction to New Testament Textual Criticism.* Grand Rapids: Eerdmans, 1964.

Groothuis, Douglas. *Christian Apologetics: A Comprehensive Case for Biblical Faith.* Downers Grove, Il.: Intervarsity Press, 2011.

----------. *Confronting the New Age.* Downers Grove, Il: InterVarsity Press, 1998.

----------. *Truth Decay.* Downers Grove, Il.: Intervarsity Press, 2000.

Grudem, Wayne. *Systematic Theology: An Introduction to Biblical Doctrine.* Grand Rapids: Zondervan, 1994.

Haley, John W. *An Examination of the Alleged Discrepancies of the Bible.* 1874; rpt. Grand Rapids: Baker, 1977.

Hume, David. "Of Miracles." *An Enquiry Concerning Human Understanding*, 1758. *Eighteenth-Century English Literature.* Ed.

Geoffrey Tillotson, Paul Fussell, Jr., and Marshall Waingrow. N.Y.: Harcourt, Brace, & World, 1069: 892-903.

Jastrow, Robert. *God and the Astronomers.* NY: Warner Books, 1980.

Jeffrey, David Lyle, ed. *A Burning and a Shining Light: English Spirituality in the Age of Wesley.* Grand Rapids: Eerdmans, 1987.

Johnson, Phillip E. *Darwin on Trial.* Downers Grove, Il.: InterVarsity Press, 1991.

Koukl, Greg. *Tactics: A Game Plan for Discussing Your Christian Convictions.* Grtand Rapids: Zondervan, 2009.

Kreeft, Peter, and Ronald Tacelli. *Handbook of Christian Apologetics.* Downers Grove, Il.: InterVarsity, 1994.

Lewis, C. S. *The Abolition of Man.* N.Y.: MacMillan, 1947.

----------. *The Last Battle.* N.Y.: HarperCollins, 1956.

----------. *Mere Christianity.* N.Y.: MacMillan, 1943.

----------. *Miracles: A Preliminary Study.* N.Y.: MacMillan, 1947.

----------. *The Problem of Pain.* N.Y.: MacMillan, 1940.

----------. *Surprised by Joy: The Shape of my Early Life.* N.Y.: Harcourt, Brace, and World, 1955.

Little, Paul. *Know Why You Believe.* Wheaton: Victor Books, 1967.

MacDonald, Lee Martin. *The Biblical Canon: Its origin, Transmission, and Authority.* Peabody, MA: Hendrickson, 2007.

MacNicol, Nicol, ed. *Hindu Scriptures: Hymns from the Rigveda, Five Uphanishads, The Bagavadgita.* London: Everyman's Library, 1948.

McDowell, Josh. *The New Evidence that Demands a Verdict: Evidence I & II Fully Updated in One Volume to Answer Questions Challenging Christians in the 21st Century.* Nashville: Thomas Nelson, 1999

Metzger, Bruce M. *The Canon of the New Testament: Its Origin, Development, and Significance.* Oxford: Clarendon, 1987.

----------. *The Text of the New Testament: Its Transmission, Corruption, and Restoration.* 3rd ed. N.Y.: Oxford University Press, 1992.

*Mining for God: A Search for Ancient Truth in a Modern World.* Ed. and Dir. Brandon McGuire. White Sail Films, n.d. DVD.

Montgomery, John Warwick. *History and Christianity.* Downers Grove, Il.: InterVarsity Press, 1965.

Moreland, J. P. *Love God with All Your Mind.* Colorado Springs: NavPress, 1997.

----------. *Scaling the Secular City.* Grand Rapids: Baker, 1987.

Morison, Frank. *Who Moved the Stone?* Downers Grove, Il.: Inter Varsity Press, n.d.

Nash, Ronald H. *Life's Ultimate Questions: An Introduction to Philosophy.* Grand Rapids: Zondervan, 1999.

Packer, J. I. and Thomas C. Oden. *One Faith: The Evangelical Consensus.* Downers Grove, Il.: InterVarsity Press, 2004.

Pearcey, Nancy. *Finding Truth: Five Principles for Unmasking Atheism, Secularism, and other God Subsitutes.* Colorado Springs: David C. Cook, 2015.

----------. *Total Truth: Liberating Christianity from its Cultural Captivity.* Wheaton: Crossway, 2004.

Piper, John, and Wayne Grudem, eds. *Recovering Biblical Manhood and Womanhood: A Response to Evangelical Feminism.* Westchester, IL.; Crossway, 1991.

Powell, Doug. *Holman Quick Source Guide to Christian Apologetics.* Nashville: Holman Reference, 2006.

Ross Hugh. *The Creator and the Cosmos: How the Greatest Scientific Discoveries of the Century Reveal God.* Colorado Springs: NavPress, 1995.

----------. The Fingerprint of God: Recent Scientific Discoveries reveal the Identity of the Creator. Orange, Ca.: Promise Publishing Co., 1991

Sayers, Dorothy L. *The Man Born to be King: A Play-Cycle on the Life of our Lord and Saviour Jesus Christ.* Grand Rapids: Eerdmans, 1944.

Schaeffer, Francis. *Genesis in Space and Time: The Flow of Biblical History.* Downers Grove, IL: InterVarsity Press, 1972.

----------*The God Who is There: Speaking Historic Christianity into the Twentieth Century.* Downers Grove, Il.: Inter-Varsity Press, 1968.

----------. *He is There and He is not Silent.* Wheaton: Tyndale, 1972.

Strobel, Lee. *The Case for a Creator.* Grand Rapids: Zondervan, 2004.

----------. *The Case for Christ.* Grand Rapids: Zondervan, 1998.

----------. *The Case for Faith.* Grand Rapids: Zondervan, 2014.

Wallace, J. Warner. *God's Crime Scene: A Cold-Case Detective Examines the Evidence for a Divinely Created Universe.* Colorado Springs: David C. Cook, 2015.

----------. *Cold Case Christianity.* Colorado Springs: David C. Cook, 2013.

Wenham, John W. *Christ and the Bible.* Downers Grove, IL: InterVarsity Press, 1972.

Williams, Donald T. "Anselm and Aslan: C. S. Lewis and the Ontological Argument." *Touchstone: A Journal of Mere Christianity* 27:6 (Nov.-Dec. 2014): 36-39.

----------. *Credo: Meditations on the Nicene Creed.* St. Louis: Chalice Press, 2007.

----------. *Deeper Magic: The Theology behind the Writings of C. S. Lewis.* Baltimore: Square Halo Press, 2016.

----------. *An Encouraging Thought: The Christian Worldview in the Writings of J. R. R. Tolkien.* Cambridge, OH: Christian Publishing House, 2018.

----------. "Identity Check: Are C. S. Lewis's Critics Right, or Is His 'Trilemma' Valid?" *Touchstone: a Journal of Mere Christianity* 23:3 (May-June 2010): 25-29.

----------. *Inklings of Reality: Essays toward a Christian Philosophy of Letters.* Lynchburg: Lantern Hollow Press, 2012.

----------. "Lacking, Ludicrous, or Logical? The Validity of Lewis's 'Trilemma.'" *Midwestern Journal of Theology* 11:1 (Spring 2012): 91-102.

----------. *Mere Humanity: G. K. Chesterton, C. S. Lewis, and J. R. R. Tolkien on the Human Condition.* Nashville: Broadman, 2006; 2nd ed., Chilicothe, OH: DeWard, 2018.

----------. *The Person and Work of the Holy Spirit.* Nashville: Broadman & Holman, 1994; rpt. Wipf and Stock.

----------. "Printing Error: Anscombe's Final Word on Lewis and Naturalism," *Touchstone: A Journal of Mere Christianity* 29:3 (May/June 2016): 20-22.

----------. "Pro: A Defense of C. S. Lewis's 'Trilemma.'" Bassham, Gregory, ed. *C. S. Lewis's Apologetics: Pro and Con.* Leiden: Brill/Rodopi, 2015: 171-89.

----------. *Reflections from Plato's Cave: Essays in Evangelical Philosophy.* Lynchburg: Lantern Hollow Press, 2012.

# GENERAL INDEX

## F



## G



## H



## I



## J



## K



## L



## M